Blue's Jokes

Blue's Jokes

ANCIENT AND MODERN,
SACRED AND PROFANE

Told and retold
by

Lionel Blue

Hodder & Stoughton
LONDON   SYDNEY   AUCKLAND

First published in Great Britain in 2001

10 9 8 7 6 5 4 3 2

British Library Cataloguing in Publication Data
A record for this book is available from the British Library

ISBN 0 340 73526 0

Printed and bound in Great Britain by Clays Ltd, St Ives plc

Hodder & Stoughton
A Division of Hodder Headline Ltd
338 Euston Road
London NW1 3BH

To my colleagues who have made me laugh
during tiresome meetings.

*'In this entire discussion no one has mentioned
God once!' said a grandiloquent rabbi.*

*'Name-dropper!' whispered Rabbi Dr Fried-
lander in my ear.*

To the doctors, nurses and specialists who kept
my spirits up. And to a fellow patient, a lady,
who exclaimed as I passed along the ward,
attached to my saline drip, 'What wonderful
legs you've got, Rabbi!' It did me
a power of good.

Contents

About This Book

The jokes, stories and riddles in this book are ones I have heard exchanged, whispered and laughed over at clergy and ecumenical meetings, have read surreptitiously and passed on at tedious lectures, have been told by strangers while shopping at supermarkets, or have overheard in cafes or at marriages, ordinations and wakes. Many are too funny to be in the best of taste. But they remain in. They are part of human life and if you ask, 'How can he include that, being a clergyman himself?' I can only reply that religion has suffered from too much good taste (or cowardice) and the hidden cost of such good taste (or cowardice) is irrelevance to people as they are, with the minds, spirits and bodies that God gave them. Healthy bawdy doesn't hurt people as much as hypocrisy.

There are only a limited number of basic jokes in the world but there are as many variations on them as there are tellers. I have called these 'Blue's Jokes' because they have linked up with my own life experience and quite simply they enlighten me or make me laugh even when I repeat them to myself, which I do quite often, as I wake up, as I queue up, as I lie in hospital or when I need to chase away my 'blues'. Some of them are mine and modern, like those about my mother – though she was pretty ancient. The rest are older and their roots and retelling go back very far. I hope some of them will enlighten you and make you laugh. I have left some blank pages at the end so

1

that you can use this as the basis for your own collection of original material.

The jokes and anecdotes contain subversive but perhaps necessary criticisms of the ecclesiastical establishment. The latter would do well to ponder them because they indicate what ordinary people really think and not what they ought to think. There is certainly plenty of material for sermons in them because they accept the tragicomedy of human life with the some of the bitterness and aggression transformed into charity and laughter. Some of the humour is very black indeed but so is the pain of the Holocaust or of long-term unemployment, which they try to alleviate. For many (including me) they are one of the ways in which we dare touch such wounds. So I have not tried to be nice and exclusive but relevant and inclusive. Spirituality is not an escape from life but the courage to re-enter it, swear at it but face it.

But above all, jokes should be enjoyed on some level or other. Enjoyment is not something most of us, or our religions, are very good at. People who are only too willing to recount their sins to God, as if he had never heard such things before, are at a loss when trying to remember and thank God for all their own good deeds and the nice things that happened to them. Good comedies are rarer than good tragedies. As a preacher I know how much easier it is to make people cry than to make them smile.

The therapeutic function of jokes has become clear to me in hospital wards and waiting rooms and in therapy sessions when the therapist or analyst is not so insecure that she or he can't laugh. (A lot of the material presented by the patient is really very funny and sometimes hilarious.) Humour-coated self-criticism and self-knowledge are much easier to digest. Humour takes away the aggression and self-hatred when administering or receiving criticism and makes them easier to swallow without psychic indigestion.

At a routine meeting, I sat back and listed these uses of humour. I've set them out higgledy-piggledy as they occurred to me. Perhaps one day I'll attach footnotes and construct a thesis out of them. I'd like to be a rabbi with a second doctorate, like scholars in Central Europe (my first doctorate is honorary).

A few of the jokes involving my family are new but the great majority are not. No one knows the original authors of jokes. They are variations on classics told many times before and which were really meant for retelling not rewriting. They are what remains of one of the fast disappearing oral traditions, which are less primitive and more sensitive than we realise – as this anecdote indicates.

Abie was invited to a meeting of rabbis and after the last resolutions were debated, his friend said blissfully as the brandy was brought round: 'Now it's time for the old favourites.'

Abie listens with anticipation.

A man gets up and shouts, 'Number 3'. There is restrained applause with some giggles.

Then another gets up and calls out, 'Number 5'. There is laughter all round.

Yet another gets up and shouts, 'Number 12 chaps'. Everyone titters.

'I don't understand,' says Abie. 'Are these jokes?'

'Sure,' says his friend. 'There's no point in telling them in full, we've heard them too many times before, so we give them numbers instead.'

'I'll try,' thinks Abie. So he gets to his feet and calls out, 'Number 8'. There is dead silence from the gathering.

'What went wrong?' asks Abie, upset.

'Sorry, but you just didn't tell it so well, Abie,' says his friend, shaking his head.

Jokes work like the minimizer and maximizer buttons on my processor. They diminish failure, anxiety and despair by so exaggerating them that they make them ridiculous, like the distorting mirrors once found in fairgrounds. They help you accept the criticism of other people and your own self-criticism because they don't assault you with it. They also help you criticise your religion so that God is allowed to grow up with you. They help you express your anger and laugh at it at the same time. They don't run away from our God-created bodies and their functions – their hair, smells, needs and contortions. They can break the tension of fraught meetings. They can expose the paradoxes of being human. Life certainly doesn't behave according to our logic nor does God behave according to any theology. They can teach you to accept what you can't change and to cope as creatively as you can with seemingly dead-end situations. They can show you how to deal with the most serious subjects without serious consequences. (There were jokes in the Warsaw Ghetto. Hitler was referred to as Horowitz. And there were subterranean jokes behind the Iron Curtain that defied the Stasi.) They can help you face threatening and dangerous situations. They can join together your sexuality and your spirituality in a way that most sermons don't dare to. They teach you that the world is not changed by laughing nor by crying so you might as well laugh.

Many of my stories have a Jewish background. This is my own background and is therefore understandable. But since they concern themselves with something more fundamental than being a Jew, Christian, agnostic or atheist, that is with being a human being, they are not difficult to translate into your own background, whatever it may be. Laughter is universal even though the culture or belief system it arises from is not.

Humour can be profound. Jokes are not just joking matters and what seems light can support a life. When editing and composing the Sabbath volume of the liturgy with Rabbi Professor Jonathan Magonet, I am pleased we managed to include some lines of Bud Flanagan, the comedian. Those lines reminded me of a story told to me by my teacher in Jewish mysticism.

When a great Talmudic rabbi visited the local market, he bumped into the prophet Elijah (a popular spirit guide of rabbis) among the tradesmen and stallholders puffing their wares. 'Who here has a chance of eternal life?' he asked him. Elijah pointed to some buskers, entertaining the crowd for pennies. 'They have the gift of eternal life,' said the prophet. The startled rabbi visited them. They were not the candidates he had expected. 'What do you do that earns you the reward of eternal life?' he asked them. They looked as puzzled as him. 'We just try to make sad people laugh,' they said, 'and when we see

*a quarrelling couple we tell them jokes to make them
happy with each other.'*

I wish I could do the same. Life isn't easy and most people
deserve a medal for surviving.

1

Have You Got Problems?

'You look awful, Jackie,' said his lawyer friend. 'What's the problem?'

'It's like this,' said Jackie dolefully and he set out the details of the case between him and his client.

'You haven't got a thing to worry about,' said his friend. 'It's such a clear case, how can you have a problem?'

'That was my client's side of the story that I explained,' answered Jackie, now more doleful than ever.

'Boy, have you got a problem!' agreed his friend sadly and whistled.

Depression

For many years I suffered from depression. I couldn't get out of bed till lunchtime or draw the curtains or answer the telephone and many of you are in the same boat. Gradually I managed to emerge from the wreck. I don't think I'll ever be completely free from depression or anxiety but the following have for practical purposes 'cured' me — sensible, contemplative religion, analysis and therapy, work and having to earn my living, a dog, ageing and jokes.

This is an ancient joke from the East European Jews, which helped me and others, though I don't really understand why because it's about a depressing situation and the joke is more depressing than the situation. But told on the radio it did stop depressives who were listening from diving back under the duvet in the morning and helped them giggle while they made themselves their first cuppas and hesitantly launched themselves into life.

> *Everything has gone wrong for Cohen. His wife has left him, his children have gone to the dogs and his business has gone bankrupt. Even the slice of toast he makes for breakfast falls to the floor. Sadly he picks it up and then, startled, notices that it's fallen BUTTERED SIDE UP. Trembling with hope, he wraps the toast in a napkin and rushes to his rabbi.*
>
> *'Rabbi, rabbi,' he shouts, 'you know how bad it's been with me over the last few years but look at this piece of toast. This morning it fell BUTTERED SIDE UP. Is it a sign from heaven that at long last my luck has changed?'*
>
> *'This is a very complex question, Mr Cohen,' answered the rabbi, stroking his beard, in deep thought. 'I shall have to research it with other rabbis, with chief rabbis, with ecumenical clergy. Come back in a week's time and I'll tell you.'*
>
> *In a week's time Mr Cohen returned. 'Rabbi, rabbi, I'm the man whose toast fell BUTTERED SIDE UP. Was it a sign from heaven that my luck has changed?' His voice became shrill with hope.*
>
> *'I'm so, so sorry,' said the rabbi sadly, 'but it was a dreadful, dreadful mistake.' His voice hardened and became brisk. 'You buttered the wrong side that's all.'*

The following may be the worst joke in the world. I heard it first many years ago when I was depressed and it shocked me into giggling irritation, my first giggle for months. But be careful – it might increase your depression or cause an explosion of anger. To make it more palatable I have shortened it down considerably. If you read the last line first, you will have spoilt it for yourself. It's a sort of kill or cure joke. If you don't feel strong enough just ignore it and read about anxiety instead.

This chap was in deep depression. On the way home he moodily looked into a pet shop window. He knew the owner and on impulse went in and confided in him.

'You're too lonely and that's your trouble,' said his friend. 'What you need is a nice pet you can talk to and who will keep you company. Now what about this parrot here. Polly's a fine talker and would do just the job. And I'll tell you what. I'll throw in her perch free if you take her.'

The depressed man saw a gleam of hope and bought her, cash down.

When he got home and sat down for supper he and Polly had a wonderful conversation. He blew kisses at her and she cawed back. They were entranced with each other. He hadn't felt so good for months.

The next morning he raced down the stairs to have breakfast with his new parrot friend. But alas, Polly lay on her back with her feet stuck in the air, stone dead. The poor man was overwhelmed with grief; thoughts of suicide and of joining Polly flitted through his mind. But then he remembered the counsel of his psychotherapist. 'I must not be defeated,' he said to himself. 'I must make something positive out of this tragedy.'

A thought occurred to him. 'I know what. I'll make myself some parrot jam. Haven't tasted good parrot jam for years.' Well, he made the jam and shakily sat down for breakfast, smearing the jam over the bread. It tasted foul and in a fit of temper he threw the pot of jam out of the window into the garden and wept.

About two weeks later, gloomily looking at the garden, he suddenly saw that carnations were growing where the parrot jam had landed. He couldn't believe his eyes and thought he was going mad.

He rushed to the pet shop and, shaking with nerves, explained the situation to his old friend. The pet shop owner comforted him saying 'There, there! I wouldn't worry about it. I'm sorry about Polly and I'm sorry the jam was so awful but the carnations are just a complete coincidence. These things happen. Look, try another pet! What about this hamster here? It's a friendly creature. Just put your finger into its cage and watch it play with it. The depressed man did just that and was enchanted by it.

'I know what a terrible time you've been having,' said the pet shop owner, 'so I'll throw in the little one's cage if you buy it.' This the man did, praying for a better result this time.

And at first all was couleur de rose. *While he supped, the hamster ran around in a wheel and played with its ball and the depressed man was actually laughing.*

The next morning he raced downstairs to play with his pet and to his horror tragedy had struck again. The poor little beast lay on its back with its feet in the air, as dead as Polly.

Have You Got Problems?

Once again the man almost succumbed to suicidal thoughts. But remembering the advice of his therapist he braced himself against defeat. 'I shall make jam out of that hamster,' he courageously asserted. 'I haven't tasted jam like that for years. I shall not be defeated by coincidences.'

So he made the jam, spread it on his toast, tasted it and spat it out. It was even worse than the parrot jam. In a frenzy he threw the jam into the garden and wept once again.

About a fortnight later he fearfully looked at his garden through a window and shook with terror. There, where he'd thrown the new jam, roses were growing. He thought, poor chap, he was going mad!

He rushed to the pet shop once again to tell the pet shop owner the whole story. This could no longer be coincidence. The two of them considered together all the events in this curious story, the deaths of both animals, completely unrelated, the dreadful jams that they had been turned into and, strangest of all, the carnations and roses that had grown out of them in the depressed man's garden.

The pet shop owner shook his head from side to side in thought. 'I don't understand it either,' he said. 'To be honest, I've never heard the likes of it. You're right, it must be more than coincidence.' Again he shook his head, this time in disbelief. 'Everyone knows,' he said, 'you get TULIPS FROM HAMSTERJAM.'

Anxiety

Say you're like me and still have to go back home five times to check you've turned the gas off and let the dog in and not vice versa. This therapeutic joke was told to me by a rabbi who was also a counsellor so he ought to know. I always use the catchphrase at the end to remind myself that I can turn my anxiety the other way round or inside out.

Mrs Shapiro comes down in the morning and finds her husband crying. He's sobbing his heart out. 'Darling,' she says, 'why are you crying?'

Her husband sobs again, 'Because I haven't slept a wink last night,' he wails.

'And why didn't you sleep a wink darling?'

'Because I owe that Garfinkel next door a hundred pounds and I can't pay it.' He then bursts into tears again.

'Don't worry' his wife says, 'I'll deal with it.'

'But how can you deal with it? You haven't got a hundred pounds either,' he says, astonished.

'You watch,' she said, marched over to the window, threw it open and shouted, 'Garfinkel!' A little face appeared at the window next door. 'Yes, Mrs Shapiro, what do you want?' said the face. 'You know my husband owes you a hundred pounds,' she said. The little face nodded. 'Well he can't pay it!' she shouted. She then shut the window with a bang, marched over to her husband, clapped her hands and said comfortably, 'Now I've dealt with it.'

'But how have you dealt with it?' said her husband, bemused.

'Ah,' she said nonchalantly, 'he should worry!'

So if you think you're responsible for everything, don't be a megalomaniac and think you're God, just say to yourself, 'He should worry!' It really helps. Another phrase that helped me, I heard when visiting a friend.

> *A young man was distractedly saying the things that most young people say: 'My parents don't understand me – they're bourgeois.' You may have said them yourself. I certainly have. My friend calmly carried on playing patience during this adolescent outburst, merely adding kindly, 'Don't take it too heavy dearie, don't take it too heavy.'*

When I die and if I have a tombstone, I should like those words engraved on it. Also, in the unlikely event of possessing a coat of arms I should like those words as my motto. Why the above joke works, again I'm not quite sure, but it does. It is another classic from the Jews of Eastern Europe.

Now the following are not jokes, just thoughts, but they help me with anxiety too. Perhaps they can help you. I think of my mother's cousins who died or disappeared during the Holocaust. They would think my present anxieties heaven! The therapy that works best with me is work. Don't worry about which work or what type of work, just get down to any work – writing, sorting out single socks (a man's problem more than a woman's), making soup, clearing out a drawer, painting by numbers etc. Don't be a snob! One kind of work will lead to another and release you from your inner persecutor. Make a list of all the things you have ever worried about and then tick off those that actually happened. You may find that it's only the things that we don't worry about that happen. This may be worrying of course, but in a different sort of way.

Our anxieties can be like superstitions or a way in which we punish ourselves because we don't think we deserve happiness. (Once again an old childhood throwback.) Isn't it time to stop punishing yourself? We lived with anxieties during the last war when I grew up. Common-sense humour took the worry out of a lot of them. This joke must have been born in the air-raid shelters.

> *The air-raid siren has sounded and the husband is shouting to his wife to come down to the shelter fast. 'But I'm looking for my false teeth,' she wailed. 'Darling,' he pleaded, 'they're dropping bombs not blintzes.' (Blintzes are little east European cheese puffs I used to like eating with sugar and sour cream.)*

When the Stock Market Goes Down

If you remember these maxims at least you won't feel surprised:

- ☀ what goes up must come down!
- ☀ there's no such thing as a free lunch;
- ☀ the devil is in the small print – read it before not after;
- ☀ it's happened to everybody else, and to a lot of people much worse off than you, so why should you be different?
- ☀ quite often it's only figures in an account book without

much relation to your happiness or unhappiness – only
to your ego;

☀ Pascal said centuries ago that things in the world wither
and fall apart. Don't wither and fall apart with them.

Having absorbed all this you need a joke or something to
cheer you up.

*Hymie in the textile trade goes bankrupt in the stock
market crash of 1929. Unable to cope he decides to
crash too. He jumps from his office on the fortieth floor
of a skyscraper. As he whizzes past the windows of his
rivals, he bellows helpfully through them, 'Fur collars
and trimming for autumn fashions'. Nice of him!*

*Two friends meet. 'I'm so sorry about the fire in your
factory. I cried and cried,' says one sadly. 'My thoughts
are with you, dear friend.' A tear runs down his cheek.*
  *'Shush. Keep your tears till next Wednesday then!'
whispers his dear friend furtively.*

Failure

One of my teachers said, 'Mr Blue, your successes may make you clever but only your failures will make you wise.' And he was right. Without failures and problems we would not know what it's like to be at the other end of the stick. Failure is the way most of us come to compassion, mercy and charity. Now in a yuppie, competitive society, failure has become a dirty word. People employ special publicity agents to prepare their CVs so that no hint of failure appears. But spiritually speaking our failures can be precious because God may prefer to speak to us through them rather than through our successes. Therefore, don't throw them away or hide them from yourself! They might have very important things to tell you.

Liverpool, in the years I knew it, was not a successful town. It never caught up with the glitz of nearby Manchester and unemployment was rife. But for me it was a kind of University of Life. I learnt not just how to make Connie Onnie butties (sandwiches of blotting paper bread with a filling of condensed milk) and blind scouse but also how to get rid of my bad vibes through jokes, so that they didn't poison my soul. The humour could be black.

A man stands by the parapet next to the Mersey and addresses a small crowd gathered round him. 'I've had enough of life,' he says. 'I don't want any of you to try and save me. I'm going to pack it all in.' He throws off his coat and his shoes and dives into the black water.

Another man at the edge of the parapet immediately throws off his coat and shoes. Someone helps him on to

*the parapet and he dives in and swims towards the first.
As he gets near him, the first shouts, 'Don't save me! I
don't want to be saved. I've had enough.' The second
man replies, 'I don't want to save you mate. I just want
to know where you work!'*

When I returned to Liverpool, someone had given the story
an ending with an even blacker twist.

*When the second man went to the factory where the
first one worked, he found the job had already been
taken by the man who had helped him onto the parapet!*

You can't get much blacker than that! But it still turned
tragedy into a sort of comedy. I liked the caustic good
humour of Liverpool. It was a refreshing change from the
chichi of 'make a fast buck' London. One drizzling night sitting in a station, waiting for a train, you might hear a conversation like this:

*'What would you like me to play on my music centre,'
said the refined barmaid, trying to improve the tone of
her bar.*

'Play Ada,' replied her customers.

*'You mean Aida,' she said coyly, correcting them
while lifting her glass of Guinness with a crooked finger.*

*'No!' said one of them, 'You know the one we mean,
"Ay dere, you wid de smile in yer eyes."'*

And here's yet another bit of Liverpool scouse:

A taxi driver driving round Paddy's wigwam (the remarkable Roman Catholic cathedral there) looked up and saw some clerics gloomily inspecting the roof.

'Don't jump, reverend sirs,' he shouted up tearfully as he whizzed round the Cathedral. 'It can't be as bad as that. Try a prayer!'

Don't despise these stories. Liverpool was going through a bad time when I knew it and together with butties, carbohydrate pies and battered chocolate bars fried in chip shops they kept it afloat, which is the purpose of jokes. Now here's a story in a different style. It's very Slav, very Jewish and very sad.

It was announced in a village in Poland that the first Jewish trapeze artist was going to jump from a high wire into a barrel of water. Before he jumped, the lights went down in the crowded tent and the Yiddish daredevil in fancy pants addressed the crowd below.

'Look!' he said, 'Don't you recognise me? I'm your old friend Izzy. We played together as children. You know my wife, Becky. Such a gentle, kind woman. She loves me and I love her. And remember our children, so well behaved. Your children play with them and we make tea for all of them together.'

'Now, do you really want me to jump?' he asked hopefully.

My mother and I used to look at nature films together on the TV. After watching one animal eat her mate after being inseminated by him, my mother very understandably exclaimed,

Have You Got Problems?

'Couldn't it have been organised better, Lionel! Don't they give you the answer in your seminary?' Well, they didn't. They didn't know either! Human failures they were good at, divine failures they didn't dare touch.

But this joke does and the answer is not unreasonable, especially if you're of a fundamentalist disposition. It was provided by my father who was not a theologian but a tailor.

> *'Harry, make me up this suit in six days. I need it for a wedding.'*
>
> *'Not possible,' said my father who needed the work but was a perfectionist. 'I'd need six weeks at the least.'*
>
> *'Look, Harry, if God made the world in six days, surely you can make up a suit!'*
>
> *'And look at the mess he made of it!' replied my father looking down his nose.*

Honesty – the Gritty Value

Not a popular virtue – especially on a cold Monday morning. All of us prefer warming, sticky virtues like love and kindness and helping old people across the road (make sure you take them in the direction they want to go!) and being kind to all small animals except rats and such like. But honesty is needed to differentiate between magic and religion. The former is about making the universe do your will and the latter about 'Thy will be done'. I am no believer in magic. I don't know of any mantra or prayer that can get us out of the consequences of our actions or the necessities of the world. If you know of any, you can tell me. I am a member of the post-Holocaust generation and I think of all the prayers – among the sincerest of the world – which must have been said in the closed wagons to the camps and which were not answered in any way we can tell. This is hard stuff for a cold Monday morning and the only way to get such craggy virtues over and not make your listeners switch off is to tell them in the form of a joke. So here are some about that uncomfortable virtue, self-honesty.

A man goes into a bar. 'Four separate tots of whisky, barman, please!' The barman becomes more and more puzzled as he sees the man drink each one in turn. On the next Saturday night the same thing happens and the barman can't resist asking why he orders four separate tots of whisky.

'It must look rather odd,' says the man, 'but it's quite simple really. I used to come to this pub with my three brothers and we used to celebrate every Saturday night with a whisky each. But you know how it is. Families disperse and I'm the only one left around here now. But on Saturday nights I still come in, order four whiskies and remember each of my brothers as I drink them one by one.'

'Thank you so much for telling me,' said the barman, deeply moved. And the following Saturday night he smiles as he pours out the separate tots.

The Saturday night following the man comes in as usual. 'Three tots of whisky, barman, please!' he orders.

The barman looks shocked. 'Oh, sir, has anything happened to one of your brothers?' he asks fearfully.

'Oh no!' says the man. 'They're all doing fine. It's me.

I've joined the AA and have just stopped drinking, that's all!'

A man stands on the parapet of London Bridge wondering whether to jump off and end it all. After all, his wife has left him, taking the children, and his business has gone bankrupt. As these thoughts go through his mind a fluting, genteel voice suddenly breaks in. 'I wouldn't do that if I were you,' it says.

Wheeling around he sees an old lady clad in charity shop cast-offs with two plastic bags by her side containing her few possessions – the kind of derelict you see outside London stations.

'Who are you and what business is it of yours?' says the man huffily.

'I'm a fairy,' she says gently, 'a good fairy and I could give you three wishes.'

Since most of us are suckers for magic, the man says, 'You mean you could get my wife back and my children back and even my business?'

'Sure, that's no problem,' she replied sweetly. 'And all we fairies want is a loving embrace from a human being.'

'Well,' he said grudgingly, 'that can be arranged.' And he goes up to her and they go into a clinch.

When it is all over, she sighs and pokes him in the ribs. 'By the way,' she adds, 'how old are you?'

'Thirty-nine,' he replies.

'Thirty-nine,' she giggles, 'and he still believes in the fairies.'

Deceiving oneself or others, which is bad, should not be confused with tact, which is the opposite and permitted.

A rabbi emphasises the importance of tact to a young student of his who is training for the congregational ministry. 'I want you to break the news to Mrs Cohen that her husband passed away this morning. It was a sudden stroke and there was nothing any of us could do about it. But don't give her a stroke too by breaking the news brutally and directly. Tell her gently so that she has time to absorb the shock!' The student promises to be very, very careful.

He goes along to the Cohen home, rings the bell and a lady opens the door. 'Does the widow Cohen live here?' he asks conversationally. The lady shakes her head. 'I'm Mrs Cohen,' she says, 'but there's no widow Cohen.' 'There is now,' said the student brightly.

Curses

Lately there's been an upsurge in curious curses. They are so over the top, they topple over and what starts as anger ends in laughter. It's a good way of getting your bad vibes out of your system. It is a method used by God as well as the prophets – in the Bible both curse a lot.

Have You Got Problems?

May God arrange a big win on the pools especially for you and an even bigger family of poor relations to share it with.

May you hire a luxury holiday mansion with ten bedrooms and each room with ten beds and still not get a good night's sleep on any of them.

May all your teeth fall out except one, so that with that one you can still feel toothache!

Please God, may your son fall in love with a doctor. (Get it?)

2

Hospitals and Sickness

Cancer Therapy Waiting Room

I didn't learn a lot about medicine in hospitals but I did learn a lot about spirituality. I was very impressed by how people help each other when they themselves are in pain or anxious. Religious folk talk a lot about original sin but in hospital waiting rooms I met original virtue. I think the humour covered our mild aggression against the hospital establishment and our fear. The patients told jokes to each other that jumped in whispers round the waiting room.

The specialist said kindly to the patient waiting for his chemo, 'I wouldn't get too upset if your hair fell out, young man.'

The young man replied politely to the specialist, 'And I wouldn't get too upset if your hair fell out either, sir.'

The nurse says brightly to the old boy, 'In this world none of us can live for ever you know.'

The old man replied stubbornly, 'But I'd like to try, nurse. Don't take it badly, but if you don't mind I'd like to try.'

The doctor studies the X-rays and says gravely to his elderly patient, 'I'm afraid you have only five more minutes to live.'

'Can't you do something? Surely you can do something, doctor,' says his distraught patient, wringing his hands.

The doctor runs his hand along his jaw in thought and concentration. 'Well,' he says hesitantly, 'if you really want one, I suppose I could boil you an egg!'

Patients and Doctors

Patients are appreciative of the help they receive but they need to express some one-upmanship because they are so dependent on other people – doctors, specialists, surgeons, office staff, nurses, orderlies, even chaplains. A joke expresses their self-assertion without seeming to be ungrateful.

In a secular time doctors and specialists replace rabbis and priests. The standard cry in my family, if things didn't go right, was not for a miracle but for a second opinion. I understand this. But for doctors and specialists and their ingenuity I would have been a gonner over 40 years ago. I freely acknowledge my debt. I think it's because of this dependence that there are so many Jewish jokes about doctors. I wish I knew the jokes that doctors tell each other about patients like me. It would complete the picture.

...an dropped down, seemingly dead, in the street.

'Get a doctor, call a doctor,' his wife shouted frantically.

A doctor rushes over to examine him and then says gently, 'I'm afraid your husband is dead, Mrs Cohen.'

At this point her husband's body starts to twitch and her 'late' husband whispers hoarsely, 'No, no, I'm not dead, darling, thank God I'm alive, alive!'

He weeps as he waits for her rejoicing and congratulations.

'Don't keep interrupting,' says his wife severely, 'I want to listen to what the doctor says!'

'You're remarkably fit for a man of 55, Mr Cohen,' says the specialist.

'Who says I'm 55?' replies Mr Cohen aggressively. 'I'm 75, thanks be to God.'

'I'm so sorry,' said the specialist, 'I didn't want to tread on your toes. You must come from a very long-living family. How old was your father when he died?' he asked pacifically.

'Who said he's dead?' said Mr Cohen, offended. 'He's 95 and also doing fine, thanks be to God!'

'I seem to be putting my foot in it again and again. Please excuse me! How old then was your grandfather when he died?'

'Who said he's dead? He's 125 and getting married on Sunday, thanks be to God!'

'But Mr Cohen,' said the bemused specialist, 'if he's 125, why does he want to get married?'

'Who says he wants to, thanks be to God!'

The two Jewish grannies converse about 'women's problems'. 'You must go and see my grandson the specialist,' says one, 'He's a wonder. After you've seen him you'll feel so good again. I'll arrange an appointment. Believe me, after treatment from him, you'll feel better than you've felt for years.'

On the appointed day the second goes to the hospital to be examined. 'Come into this cubicle,' says the specialist kindly, 'and let's see what it's all about. Don't be worried. It won't hurt.'

He examines her and then, seated behind his desk, he tells her about further tests he'll have to make. She returns his smiles with a basilisk stare. She doesn't even thank him or acknowledge him. He sighs at the ingratitude but remains polite and kind.

Just as the old lady is at the door about to leave, she suddenly turns and croaks in a knowing whisper, 'Between you and me, does your grandmummy know how you make a living, young man?'

Listening – the Patient's Complaint

No patient ever feels listened to enough – the hospital staff, coping with emergencies, just haven't got the time. But listening and attention are the most precious gifts you can give to anyone who is ill – more helpful than peonies or grapes.

I've learnt a lot about listening from an Anglican priest, who put two coal bunkers together. It was his listening post, surrounded by nightclubs, bars and pick-up parlours. It opened about four in the morning and he gave his visitors his full attention – no advice unless they asked for it. To it flocked those who had not been able to find a partner and were frightened of their own loneliness. They couldn't admit that at first, of course. So some tried to knock him out, and some tried to rape him, and some stripped in front of him or tried to make love to him. They couldn't believe that he really wanted to listen to them and give them his full attention. But he did. Jokes were a bond between him and his visitors. Laughter and a giggle also unite the human race.

Another friend of mine had a breakdown and went to a psychiatric hospital. The doctors deliberated on which treatment he should have. Some of the suggestions were pretty horrific. When I visited him, I asked him if they had asked him what he thought about his problems and his situation. No, he said, only the ward orderly who poured out tea, a genial lady from the Caribbean, ever wanted to listen to him!

In my seminary I learnt to talk, preach and conduct meetings but no one taught me to listen.

The new young psychiatrist enters the staff common room, distraught. 'I'm shaking so much I can't even pick up this cup,' he says to an older colleague. 'How can you carry on eating cream eclairs after listening to their stories?'

His colleague continues munching placidly. 'Who listens?' he says.

Two friends, who haven't seen each other for years, meet in the street.

'I'm sorry but I've really got to go,' says one regretfully, anxiously consulting his watch. 'I've an appointment with my analyst. And I'm already late for my session.'

'Why worry? After all, he can't start without you,' says the other, laughing.

'Yes, but mine does, you see,' says the first simply and sighs.

'Doctor, doctor, tell me I'm imagining it and it's just a complex! I just feel that everybody ignores me!' The patient bursts into tears of self-pity.

'Next please, nurse Jones!' said the psychiatrist wearily.

Psychotherapy and Psychoanalysis

At one time these were professions invented by Jews and run by Jews for Jews. Now all the suburban middle class have caught the habit and become honorary Jews. A personal experience of the only time I was ever cajoled into the role of therapist, many decades ago:

Just as I was shutting up shop in my new synagogue, a distraught American lady was deposited on my doorstep by a taxi driver. She had hailed him in Park Lane and told him to find her a rabbi – not that easy so late at night. He had brought her to me.

Though tired, I listened to her involved and turgid story about her two husbands, her present lover and her 'dawg'. I suggested she should see her analyst, who lived in Paris, as I was neither an analyst nor a therapist and, being young and untrained, out of my depth. My rabbinical training had not prepared me for the likes of ladies like her.

'I know you won't be of much use,' she snapped, 'but you come free and I spent all my alimony cheque in Bond Street.'

It took me half an hour to find a taxi (for which I paid) to deposit her back in her natural habitat of Park Lane; she was talked out and relaxed, I was worn out and exhausted.

'What is your problem, Mr Smith?'

'Every time I dream and go up to someone in my dream that person turns into my mother. I panic and tremble.'

'And what do you do then?'

'Well, doctor, I'm so upset I get up and make myself some breakfast to restore my nerves.'

'And what do you have for breakfast?'

'Does that matter, doctor, a cup of tea and some bread, the one I like with the seeds on top.'

'How many slices of bread?' enquired the doctor urgently.

'Only one slice doctor. Is that important?'

Suddenly he sees the doctor's head shaking from side to side and a tear is running down the doctor's cheek.

'Do you call that a proper breakfast for a big, growing boy like you?' sobs the doctor reproachfully.

'What's your problem?' 'It's so complex and so strange, I scarcely know where to begin, doctor.'

'Well, why not begin at the beginning – that's the usual place.'

The patient sighs. 'OK, here goes! Well, in the beginning you see,' he said conversationally, 'I created the heavens and the earth . . . and on the seventh day I rested.'

The Patient's Point of View

Patients criticise everybody and everything. Jokes are the non-aggressive way in which they can assert themselves and keep their own side up. There are jokes even about visitors. Yes, their visits are appreciated and it's nice to know you're not forgotten but it's difficult conducting a cocktail party, minus the cocktails, round your bed. And so many grapes!

Two ladies go on a safari holiday in southern Africa. In the bush a great gorilla leaps out at them. One gets away but the gorilla grabs the other, takes her back to his cave and 'embraces' her that night, and the next morning, and the night after that. The gorilla is then so tired, he goes out foraging for food at dawn to replace his lost energy. The woman then takes the opportunity to stagger out and is soon found by some hunters. They take her to the nearest town where she is put in hospital suffering from shock. The news is in all the papers. Her friend hears about it, rushes to the hospital and sits by her bed. 'How do you feel?' she exclaims in horror. 'How should I feel?' replies her friend in tears. 'He doesn't visit. He doesn't write. No grapes...'

Chaplains aren't protected by their dog collars either.

A daughter visits her mum in the surgical ward. 'There he is down there,' exclaims her mum, pointing down the ward. 'You mark him, daughter. A saintly man of God, that's what he is, a chaplain with holy hands, daughter.'

The daughter looks at the man respectfully but then says, puzzled, 'But that ain't the chaplain, mum, that's the surgeon.'

'Hmm ... ' said her mum, 'now I come to think about it, he was pretty fresh for a chaplain!'

Nor are the hospital staff immune either.

The telephone rings in the ward. 'How can I help you?' enquires the sister politely. 'Please, I want to know how Mrs Cohen is getting on,' says the voice tremulously. 'She's doing fine,' says the sister comfortingly. 'We expect her out in a few days. Who shall I say has enquired after her?' she adds kindly.

'It's me, Mrs Cohen,' says the voice hurriedly. 'It's the only way I ever get to know how I am!' She rings off quickly.

Dying and After

Yes, jokes are made even about that too. Traditionally there is little fear of death – only of pain. The problem is this world not the next.

> *'Only a small percentage of babies ever get born, but who has the good luck to be among them?'*

As a child I became influenced by my grandfather's view about death, which was decidedly robust. An elderly great aunt had died and my grandfather decided the time had come to initiate me into the courtesies of death. Walking to the house of mourning he gave me a long disquisition about how to act among the bereaved. On arriving we found the mourners sitting on low chairs, as is the Jewish custom, looking haggard. My grandfather certainly let in some fresh air. In a booming voice he announced to all that he knew exactly how they felt because, 'I also hate losing things!' They looked at him with jaws dropped open in astonishment and a cousin quickly gave my grandfather a whisky to shut him up. On the way home grandpa gave me a long lecture on tact with the bereaved. He was mighty pleased with himself.

I must have inherited his robustness because death does still not seem to me so terrible. (Hell hardly figures in Judaism so there is little fear on that score.) Pain does, death doesn't. I once asked one of my teachers what my last judgement would be like. He said that God would take me on His knee, so to speak, and say, 'Well, Lionel, you did just as I expected – no better, no worse.' He would then tell me what my life was really about and when I saw the good I'd done and the bad I'd done and their consequences, that would be my heaven and hell. Somehow it would all work out right in the end. That is why I can take robust jokes on any subject with equanimity.

A woman's husband died and the undertakers carried the coffin carefully down the stairs. But as they got to a particularly awkward bend, the coffin slipped and ricocheted down the stairs. As the bearers rushed to pick it up, a faint cry could be heard from the coffin. They hastily broke open the lid and revived the poor man. They carried him upstairs and dosed him with a spoonful of brandy – and themselves too because they needed it as well. Well, he recovered and lived contentedly for another year before he died again.

As the coffin was taken once more down the stairs and arrived at the awkward bend, his wife piped up in a tremulous tone, 'Please, please, be very, very careful! A tragedy nearly happened just here only a year ago…'

The man lies dying. Suddenly he seems to regain consciousness. Weakly he says to his daughter beside his bed, 'I can smell your mother's own cheesecake. Get me a slice, darling, before I leave you for ever and will never taste it again!'

His daughter rushes out and returns unwillingly, 'Ma said she's terribly sorry, dad, but she's worried she won't have enough for your wake.'

Grandpa lived till nearly 100 – he never knew his age exactly, carousing, smoking and womanising till the last. But he was an exception. Usually women fare better than men with ageing. At 70 there are still a minority of men around. At 80 it's pretty much a woman's world.

An elderly couple go to inspect retirement flats at the seaside. They look one over and the wife says to her husband, 'Now this one suits me fine. Whichever of us dies first, I'll feel quite cosy here.'

The old lady is dying. The rabbi guides her through the prayers, the traditions and the rituals, supervising their performance punctiliously.

When they are all done, the old lady, in a weak voice, nervously calls to the rabbi. 'Am I permitted to have a glass of water before I die?' she asks weakly.

If you can stand it, and want to stand it, here's an even blacker bit of humour. I'm not quite sure why there are so many such jokes. I suppose they exaggerate and make fun of the grief of the situation and so make it supportable.

The father is dying and seemingly unconscious. His daughter suddenly says excitedly, 'He must want some-

thing. I can see his lips move. I'm sure he's calling to me. Daddy, I'm coming, I'm coming!'

She sits on the bed beside him cradling him. 'Oh, my God,' she says, 'he's going. It's his last breath. But he wants to say something special to me I know.' Tremblingly she puts paper and pencil before the dying man. He scribbles for a moment and then expires. 'Oh, what's dear papa's last message?' she sobs, and picks up the paper with trembling hands. It reads, 'Get off! You're sitting on my oxygen . . . '

'Yes,' said the new widow, 'my Abie really looked after me right to the end. He left me the house without a mortgage and a life policy. What a wonderful man. He even set aside the money for the funeral, for the plot of land he loved overlooking the motorway, for his coffin and even £50,000 for the stone.'

She extended her hand with its dazzling diamond ring. 'Boy, doesn't that stone glitter!' she added reverently.

Mrs Goldberg's husband is killed instantaneously when a lorry crashes into his little roadster. After the funeral the solicitor visits her. 'I didn't want to intrude on your grief,' he said to the sobbing widow, 'and I know it won't make any difference but your husband left you his life insurance worth £300,000.'

The widow sobbed again. 'Why,' she said, out of her mind with grief, 'I'd return a thousand of it, if only that would bring my Abie back to me.'

Some rabbis thought dying was like a ritual bath that washed away our sins. I hope so!

3

Sex, Being In Love
and Love

Love

Young and romantic:

> *The two girls are on the plane back from their holiday in Benidorm. One of them is distraught. 'I can't live without him,' she sobs. 'He means more to me than life. He's not a waiter really but a film director and he's going to wait for me till next summer. I must write to him immediately. Oh God, what's his name. You must remember it. It was Rinaldo or Antonio or something. I'm feeling faint. Was it Carlo? Oh dear!'*

Ancient and ageing. Many youngsters get disgusted by oldies falling in love or making love with each other. They think such things should be reserved for them. But as the span of life increases, second childhood is followed by second adolescence and it can be as deep and painful as the first time around. I've met many oldies broken by romantic love – and many sharks who prey on their feelings.

> *The old married couple lie beside each other in bed on their anniversary.*
> *'I can't help remembering your old passion,' she says to*

*her husband. You were an animal, a tiger. I remember
your embraces, your passionate kisses, your love bites...'*

    *Her husband stumbles out of bed and stumbles
towards the door. 'Oh, my darling,' his wife calls out
remorsefully, 'don't leave me! I didn't want to shame
you or make you sad...'*

    *'You haven't,' he says excitedly, 'Where are my false
teeth?'*

The above situation is optimistic and I hope she had a beautiful bite mark to keep as a souvenir. The following, which is similar, is alas not.

*The old couple lie in bed on their anniversary saying
nothing to each other for nearly half an hour. Then the
husband sighs and breaks the silence.*

    *'I understand, I understand,' he whispers compassionately. 'So you can't remember anyone else either to
dream about.'*

Perhaps the love is in the compassion. Just as sex can exist without love, the opposite is also true.

Lesbians and Gays

The jokes have become kinder in recent years.

*A man puts his arm around a girl at the holiday hotel
bar. 'Say, baby,' he says, 'what about a little hotcha in
my room tonight?'*

'Leave me alone, I'm a lesbian,' she says, proudly pointing to her badge and firmly pushing away his hand.

'That's alright by me,' he whispers seductively. 'I've no prejudices. You can tell me afterwards what's up in little old Beirut, baby!'

Two mothers meet and compare their offspring.

One says to the other, 'My son's a successful surgeon now. He has a practice in Harley Street. What's your son doing?'

'He's a homosexual,' said the other sadly and sighs.

'That's original. So where's his office?'

Here's a very black joke indeed. Matzo, for those who have never tasted it, is a thin biscuit of unleavened bread always eaten at Passover time but delicious during the rest of the year and especially with cheese.

One woman says to another 'How's your boy doing?'

'Fine,' she replies, 'he's got consulting rooms in Harley Street now. And how's things with your boy?'

'He's got Aids,' the other says sadly.

'So what do you do for him?'

'I try and feed him up,' she replies. 'In the morning I give him Matzo and cream cheese and for lunch Matzo with salt beef and for supper Matzo with smoked salmon.'

'What a wonderful Jewish mother you are,' says her friend. 'But why so much Matzo?'

'It's the only thing that goes under the door!'

Sex, Being in Love and Love

A Bit of Bawdy though not Immoral

I was urged at a dinner party to tell some jokes, unsuitable for public broadcasting. 'You can't shock us,' said the other guests merrily. I was innocent enough to believe them. I told the first, being high with wine, and the party went into deep freeze. When I opened the door, our host was rolling around the floor, purple in the face, laughing his head off. I still say my joke was not immoral, just matter of fact physical. If you're going to be pedantic about such things, the couple mentioned in it were after all married.

Two women at a party.

'My, what lovely roses!' one exclaimed enviously.

'Yes, my husband gave them to me,' the other snapped.

'And what do you do for them?'

'What do you think I do for them? What does anyone do for them?' she said in exasperation. 'I just lie down on my back in bed with my tootsies stuck up in the air.'

'Well, if you had only asked me, I'd have lent you a vase,' said the other reproachfully.

A woman walks down the street and sees clocks and watches displayed in a shop window. She enters. A traditional old Jew with ear locks is sitting behind the counter reading a religious tome. 'Please mend my watch as soon as possible,' she says.

'I know nothing about watches, madam,' says the shopkeeper brusquely.

'Then what are you?'

'A Jewish Mohel, a ritual circumciser.'

'If you're not a watchmaker then why have you set out all those misleading clocks and watches in the window?'

'You tell me, madam,' he says wearily, 'what should I put in the window?'

Here Are One or Two Over the Line

That's life! – and always has been. Even in 'ages of faith' people needed the stories of Chaucer and Rabelais. People sleep with each other for many reasons, both good and bad, to warm each other in the cold, for companionship in the darkness of the night, for money or manipulation, out of desire or domination, to have children, as a tranquiliser, to get to sleep, to enjoy companionship, for friendship or convenience, because it's less solipsist than masturbation, because they want to be closer to another human being, because physical love is an art and they want to learn it, because sex can be very funny... Bawdy jokes take the tension out of the exerci se, so feel free to enjoy the following! But one caution – do not confuse sex with love or being IN love with love. The first is a feeling in a bar, the latter a commitment and a decision. Also – most important! – do not do the night before what you will regret the morning after.

Mr Cohen bursts into his bedroom and discovers his wife in bed with his business partner.

'And what do you think you're both up to?' he says, grand and judgemental.

'Now didn't I tell you he was a fool,' his wife says conversationally to her bedmate.

'I really don't understand it!' says a puzzled lady to her lawyer. 'I've come to you because I must get to the bottom of it. I can't sleep till I know what it's all about.'

'What don't you understand?' says her lawyer.

'Well, just as I'm doing the morning housework, there's a ring at the door bell and this man asks politely, "Is your husband at home, madam?" "No," I tell him. "My husband's a conscientious hard worker, a provider and a family man. He leaves the house at six sharp and doesn't get back till after the late shift."'

'And what then?' breathed her lawyer, intrigued in spite of himself.

'Well, he then pushes open the door, throws me over his shoulder, takes me to the bedroom, and pushes me on the bed. I don't understand it!'

'I'm not sure I understand your problem myself,' said the lawyer. 'Is that all?'

'No, he comes around the same time a few days later. He asks politely, "Is your husband in madam?" and I tell him, "I told you before. My husband's a fine hard worker, a provider and a family man. He leaves the house straight after early breakfast and doesn't return home till after the night shift." And then the same thing happens. I don't understand it at all!'

'But what don't you understand?' asks the puzzled lawyer.

'Well, what's his real business with my Abie?'

A mother is talking women's talk with her daughter. 'How's life, Mum?' asked her daughter. 'OK,' replied her mother, 'but as you get older the sex bit ain't what it used to be.'

'But do you make it interesting for Dad?'

'What do you mean interesting? I do everything a decent Jewish woman should.'

'Well, do you moan for example?' asked her daughter helpfully.

'Why should I moan? Is that what he really wants?' she answered incredulously.

'Try it, Mum – what have you got to lose?'

Sadie goes home thoughtfully and says to her husband in bed, 'Hymie, do you want me to moan when we do it. Is that what you'd like?'

'Wonderful, wonderful!' said Hymie, ecstatic, and he starts fondling her and making love.

'Do you want me to moan now?' said his wife.

'No, not now, darling – later, later!'

A few minutes later his wife repeated the question. 'Do I moan now?' she asks.

'No, not now, baby – a little bit later.'

After another few minutes she asks again, tired of waiting, 'Well, do I moan now?'

'Yes, yes,' replies her husband, breathless with passion. 'Moan now! Moan now! Moan! Moan! Oh boy! Oh boy!'

'God in heaven, what a dreadful day I've had,' she sighs resignedly.

Elderly Jake and Beckie seem to have a placid, contented marriage. But one day a so-called friend of Beckie's points out a beautiful, young woman in a mink coat. 'That,' she says with a wicked smile, 'is your husband's mistress. Everyone knows about it and where her coat came from.'

That night Beckie could not keep quiet. 'Jake,' she said, 'is it true you've got a mistress? Aren't I good enough for you any more after all these years?' And she burst into tears.

Her husband cuddled her and soothed her. 'Baby,' he said, 'if you're in the big time like me, you just have to have a mistress. It's like having an office in Park Lane and wearing designer underwear. It doesn't mean a thing. Every successful businessman has to have one.'

Bit by bit he mollified his wife, cuddled her and she felt less threatened.

A few days later they go to a charity ball. 'Look,' says Beckie, 'that's old Harry over there but who's the woman next to him in the mink. I know it isn't his wife because she's in Paris.'

Jake looks to where she is pointing and laughs. 'That's old Harry's mistress,' he says. 'His business is also doing fine and he's got to look successful too.'

Beckie examines the woman critically. 'Our mistress is

much more glamorous in our mink than his mistress is in his,' she says proudly.

Divorce

The rabbis of old didn't go in for 'guilty parties'. Who knows why a marriage goes wrong? It can go sour over such small things. That is why the groom smashes a glass at a Jewish wedding. It can take years to create a fine glass, but one angry word can smash it in a moment. It is a warning at the end of the marriage service and its message is 'Be careful!' Even in a row do not say what is unforgiveable. Also do not let your partner walk out too many times. One night she or he might not come back.

The couple have gone to see the rabbi to apply for a religious divorce. The husband tells his side of the story. 'You're right,' says the rabbi. Then the wife presents her side of the story. 'And you're so right too,' says the rabbi.

A bystander, who has been listening, protests. 'But if he's right, how can she be right as well!' 'And you're also so right,' said the rabbi, stroking his beard.

And I think the rabbi was so right too! Administering a divorce court for my religious community, I often thought that if life was only a simple struggle between truth and lies or between right and wrong, there would be less of a problem. But between truth and truth is very complex.

A yuppie divorce:

'I'm getting you a diamond bracelet for our anniversary, honey,' said the husband.

'What I would really prefer, darling, is a divorce,' she replied languidly.

'I don't think I could manage something so expensive, honey,' he answered tenderly.

An elderly couple come before the rabbi petitioning for a religious divorce. 'How old are you?' he asked, astonished. 'I'm 97 and she's 93,' said the husband. 'But why did you leave it so long?' asked the puzzled rabbi. 'We wanted to wait till the children died.'

'I must have a divorce as soon as possible,' said the wife to the rabbi. 'I can't bear living with him a moment longer. He's a boor, a stupid brute, an ignoramus.' 'But you've been together so long, why have you waited so many years before deciding?' asked the astonished rabbi. 'Because I only got the Etiquette and Manners Book out of the library last week and just finished it yesterday. I couldn't read it quicker, I'm not a fast reader like you, rabbi!'

For many years I was in charge of my organisation's Beth Din – its canon law court. I was appointed, one of my colleagues told me, 'because you like saying yes to things' which was most imaginative of them. Though I am not an establishment type I suddenly became responsible for its good running and for over fifteen years dealt with all the things that aren't supposed to happen in Jewish suburbia but of course do – marrying 'out', conversion, divorce and rows.

Divorces are sad things, even if there are no children and the partners stay fond of each other. My secretary used to comfort our applicants with coffee and home-made cake and the applicants used to cheer me up because often I was sadder than them.

A man goes into a bookshop and asks to be shown the cookery books. He selects an expensive, glossy one with pictures illustrating festival foods.

'What a lovely book,' said the lady at the check-out admiringly, 'and so useful too as Christmas is coming. Are you a cook? The best ones these days are men – just look at the TV.'

'Oh no,' said the man, 'it's not for me, it's my present for my wife.'

'What a sensible gift. I'm sure she'll love it,' replied the check-out girl enthusiastically.

'I wonder,' said the man, smiling to himself. 'She was so looking forward to a dinner dance at the Dorch you know.'

4

Happy Families

Children

Children figure largely on Jewish agendas. There may be a theological basis for it. They are one generation closer to the coming of the Messiah and the end of the Jewish Problem. Who knows – they might witness that coming themselves? But whatever the reason, there is an uncommon degree of idolisation. Jewish children in my experience receive lots of love but little childhood. Proof? Me!

Four ladies sit round the bridge table on the cruise boat.

'Oh, my God!' says one.

'I can't sleep thinking about it,' sobs another.

'I worry myself sick,' whispers the third.

'Now we've discussed the children,' said the fourth firmly, 'who's for tea and Black Forest Gateau with whipped cream?'

Two women met on holiday. 'Thank God I'm away from that family of mine. How many children have you got?'

'I haven't got any. We're dinkies,' said the other sadly, 'Double Income No Kids.'

'So how do you get your aggravation?'

But children can also bring their mothers great consolation.

A lady congratulates another on her daughter's marriage. 'To a dentist I hear,' she said. 'That must be nice for you!'

'It only lasted two months,' said the other gloomily, 'and then they got divorced. 'She married the co-respondent, her lawyer.' She sighed.

'Well, I'll congratulate you on her marriage to the lawyer then,' said her friend cheerfully.

'Oh, that didn't last either,' the other said sadly. 'She felt stressed, consulted a doctor and then married him.'

'Oh my dear', exclaimed the other. 'How lucky you are! A dentist, a lawyer and then a doctor! How lucky you are! So much satisfaction from just one daughter!'

Mrs Cohen takes her little Isaac to the psychiatrist. After examining him, the analyst calls in Mrs Cohen. 'There's nothing wrong with your little Isaac,' he says reassuringly, 'apart from a somewhat overdeveloped Oedipus Complex.' Mrs Cohen beams at him. 'Such a relief, doctor!' and clutches her son to her bosom. 'Oedipus-Shmoedipus, what do I care so long as my little Isaac loves his mummy!'

A woman wanders through India from one holy man to another. But she is restless, never finding what she

*seeks. Each time she asks, 'Is there one even holier?'
'Sure,' they tell her, 'but he's in a monastery on a snow-
bound peak in the Himalayas and you would need mountain guides.' 'Get me mountain guides!' she says calmly.
'Money is no object in my search for the holiest.'*

*So with their help she arrived at a monastery far
above the snow line. 'You cannot see the Great Guru,'
the monks there told her. 'He is in the deepest trance
and his eyes look only inward.'*

*'Just let me into his presence,' she begs, 'that will be
enough.'*

*Reluctantly the monks do so, telling her he would not
even be aware of her presence so deep was his contem-
plation.*

*For a few minutes she gazes at the saint whose eyes
are turned inward. 'Abie,' she says firmly 'now you've
gone too far! And you need a fresh loincloth,' she sniffs
critically, 'I'll iron one for you.'*

A personal note. My father decided I would be an athlete
like him and my mother was equally determined I must
become a solicitor like the ones she knew in her office. I
liked this story because it reminds me of my own mother
when I rang up to tell her I was going to become a rabbi.
There was a pregnant silence. Her feelings must be too
great for utterance, I thought with satisfaction. They were.
She said in a strangled tone. 'Lionel, you're doing it to spite
us. All our lives your father and I have been working our fin-
gers to the bone to get you out of the ghetto. And now you
get to Oxford, you jump right back into it again. You're
doing it to spite us.' She had a point because my poor father

who worked in a steamy factory during the week could no longer garden on the Sabbath so as not to offend my new found piety. Fortunately, this nasty religion never lasted with me that long. My inner voice told me what to do with it in no uncertain terms.

The three women compared notes about their children.
'Mine,' said the first, 'gave us a first hand Rembrandt for our anniversary to hang over our fireplace!'
'Mine,' said the second, 'gave me two solid silver tea services – one for milk and the other for meat. Isn't that thoughtful now?'
'But mine,' said the third proudly, 'pays hundreds of pounds to the most expensive psycho in Harley Street three times a week and guess! All they ever talk about together is me, his mummy!'

In Jewish households it is often grannies who love their children most and least manipulatively.

One granny peers into the pram while chatting to the little child's granny. She coos properly and then asks 'And how old is he?'
'He can walk now,' says the other proudly, 'but thanks be to God he'll never have to!'

The same scenario – peering into the pram at three little mites.

'What are their names?' says one granny to the other.
'They haven't got them yet,' replies the other granny,

'but it doesn't matter. This one's the accountant and that's the surgeon and that's the barrister.'

The Child Within Us

At some private times in life, the little child that lives within us, and controls more of our deeds and doings than we give it credit for, pops out and demands our attention.

It can pop out just when we are falling asleep or during a serious, weighty business meeting where it has no place or during agonised prayers or whilst making love. Tell it a joke to humour it, which should keep it quiet. What about these!

> *'Knock, knock!'*
> *'Who's there?'*
> *'Arthur.'*
> *'Arthur who?'*
> *'Ar-thermometer.'*

Or what about this hangover from the sixties?

> *'Knock, knock!'*
> *'Who's there?'*
> *'Doctor!'*
> *'Doctor who?'*
> *'Doctor Who!'*

Or:

'A French cat and an English cat tried to swim the Channel. The English cat was called One, Two, Three and the French cat, Un, Deux, Trois.'

'Which made it across?'

'The English cat of course! Because the Un Deux Trois quat' cinq.' Get it?

This is another story for the child that lives in all of us!

In Africa, some anthropologists heard of a tribe which every few years performed the mysterious Butcher Dance. Hacking their way through the jungle they located the tribe and asked the Chief if they could see it being performed.

'Sure,' he said, 'but we only do it once a year and last night was the night.'

They stayed for a year, waiting to witness the mysterious Butcher Dance, and when the time came, as dusk approached, they watched entranced as, gravely in the twilight, the tribe joined hands in a great circle.

Then the Chief shouted, 'The Butcher Dance!'

Reverently everyone extended first a foot and then a hand into the psychic circle and as the anthropologists became more excited and made copious notes, the worshippers began to chant with increasing abandon and liberation, constantly quickening, 'You putcha right foot in, you putcha right foot out...'

No, there's no anthropological or theological message – it's just fun.

Children at School

'Mummy, I don't want to go to school. They all bully me and throw things at me. Let me stay at home –please, please!'

'But darling, you've got to go to school. Everybody's got to go to school. Look, I'll come with you to the gate and make sure they don't throw things.'

'But mummy, the teachers don't like me and I know the kids all despise me because I won't play their silly games. Let me stay – please, please! They wouldn't miss me, so why must I go to school?'

'Darling, you must because you're the headmaster!'

Little Izzie is sent to religion school. When he returns his parents ask him what he has learnt and he proudly reads, with many stumbles and mistakes, the Kaddish, the prayer to commemorate dead parents. The parents faces go white and they summon little Izzie's teacher. 'How could you teach him such a prayer?' they demand.

The teacher tries to pacify them. 'You don't have to worry. You should live so long,' he says kindly, 'until your little Izzie learns it.'

'And if my Alfie starts talking to the boy next to him during lessons, give the boy sitting next to him a good hard smack.'

'But why the boy next to him?' asked the bewildered teacher.

'My Alfie's no fool. After a few times he'll get the message right enough!'

'Well,' the old rabbi asked his grandson who studied science at school, 'what did you learn today?'

'We learnt about the Relativity Theory of the great Einstein,' said the boy.

'Tell me about it,' said his grandfather, interested.

'It's like this, Grandad – if a gorgeous blond sits on your lap the hours seem like seconds and if you sit on a red hot needle the seconds seem like hours.'

The rabbi was lost in thought. 'This makes Einstein great?' he mused wonderingly.

Mothers

The telephone rings.

'Mama,' says the voice, 'I don't know what to do. The kids have to get their teeth checked and I've got to make dinner for the boss and his wife. I'm at my wits' end and feel like crying!'

'Don't cry my darling, mama will see to everything. I can get to that delicatessen on my new crutches and get that fried fish you like and I'll cancel my old people's club and make you a strudel they'll love. That's what a Yiddish mama is for.'

'Oh mama, thank you, but who's going to baby-sit during the dinner party? It's too late to get anyone.'

'It's never too late for your mama. Look, I'll come round and wash up and baby-sit. You won't have to worry about a thing.'

'Oh mama, you're so good – Mervin always says so and little Lester and Craig adore you.'

'Mervin, Lester, Craig! My son-in-law's name is Lionel and my grandchildren are Gary and Dwight. And who are you, young lady, and what number are you ringing?'

'I'm your Gloria and I'm ringing 01231234, mama.'

'My daughter's name is Esther and you've got the wrong number and woken me up! You should be ashamed of yourself.'

There was a silence at the other end of the telephone. Then the voice whimpered, 'I'm so sorry, but mama, forgive me, just tell me you're still coming?'

The young composer was struggling for inspiration in his attic study. A wonderful tune was just a whisper away. He had nearly got it when there was a tap at the door. It was his old mother.

'Darling,' she said, 'I hate you working so hard. Look, I've brought you some pickled herrings, they're good for the brains.'

His concentration snapped. 'Mama,' he said, controlling himself, 'not just now, darling. Just leave me alone, I'm on the edge of something big.'

He could hear her moaning as she went down the

stairs. After a while his concentration came back. The tune, the words were almost born.

Suddenly there was another knock at the door and his inspiration fled again. 'It's me, your mama,' she said piteously, wringing her hands. 'I've brought you those biscuits and fancies you used to like so much. You know, darling, I'd give my life for you!'

He gritted his teeth and steered her to the door and shut it firmly behind her. 'Mama,' he shouted through it, 'don't you understand? I've got to be alone.'

Gloomily he sat by his desk.

It took ten minutes before the idea once more began to surface in his mind.

Once again there was a tap at the door. 'I can't stand it, my little one, if you're angry with me. Look, here's some smoked salmon,' she whispered, 'to make peace between us,' and burst into tears.

Her son came purposefully towards her with a strange light in his eyes, a light she had never seen before. He snatched the smoked salmon, the plate, the cutlery and threw them all down the corridor and pushed his mother after them. He could hear the clatter.

He raced back to his desk. The tune, the words, everything was falling into place. He wrote furiously and then wept as he hummed the song that would be his masterpiece. 'My Yiddishe mama,' he crooned, 'I need her more than ever now!'

Although my mother would have sacrificed her life for me, she was not a true Yiddishe mama. She hated cooking and housework, being a business lady and a flapper. She danced the Black Bottom and taught me the Charleston at the London Trocadero when I was a child. She knew she wasn't a Yiddishe mama and felt guilty about it. I sussed this out early on. So just as she manipulated my guilt, I manipulated hers. In her old age (and mine) we couldn't stop laughing at the tricks we once played on each other.

> *Mrs Shapiro and her newly married daughter are having tea quietly, enjoying woman talk.*
>
> *'Ma,' says the daughter, 'what's the secret of your happy marriage? Everybody else gets divorced or something but I've never known you argue with each other once.'*
>
> *'It's simple, dear,' said her mother. 'I leave all the big decisions to your father as a wife should, like whether we join the EU or pull out of Northern Ireland or build our own missile intervention system. I just decide the small things like how we put the kids through University or pay into a pension or where we go on holiday. It's simple!'*

The Sayings of My Mother

My mother was not a witty person but she was an innocent person and curious. Her humour was quite unconscious and all the funnier for that. It arose from the fact that she said the first thing that came into her head. Few of us dare do that but my mother did. At parties I used to listen to her with awe. So did many others who couldn't believe what they were hearing, but I could.

I was just rushing out of the door when my mother stopped me. She was in her nineties but still curious about life and wanted to know where I was going.

'To the solicitor's, dear,' I replied. 'I've got to make a new will so that you and Lil (her elder sister) can live comfortably if I die first. Why,' I said encouragingly, 'you'll even be able to have tea at the Ritz!'

'Don't talk about such things,' said my mother crossly.

But next morning as I was coming down the stairs I heard her and my aunt in earnest discussion. They were both hard of hearing and booming forth. My mother was asking my aunt if she had ever been to the Ritz and what was it like?

I giggled and said, 'Good on yer ma!'

My aunt was more conventional. She was a member in good standing of an Orthodox synagogue but she had her moments too.

My friend came down in the morning and entered the empty sitting room. But he soon realised it wasn't as empty as he thought. My mother was standing stark naked behind the door.

'Hetty,' he said sternly, 'Lionel's told you you've got to dress and undress in the bedroom not the sitting room.'

'I'll remember that,' said my mother comfortably – which she wouldn't.

In the kitchen my aunt was looking for her false teeth in the rubbish bin. 'Your sister's naked in the sitting room,' said Jim, 'You'd better do something about it.'

*'She's got no shame,' said my aunt meditatively.
'Never had any.'*

Then a thought occurred to her, which cheered her up.

*'You know Jim,' she said, 'lots of men would pay good
money to see that!'*

My aunt had no money but once, when I'd complained
about my lack of it, she left her Post Office Savings Book
and her Building Society Book under my pillow telling me to
take it all. They were a generous pair. I remember as a child
my mother giving her only winter coat to a coughing cleaner
who lived round the corner in the tenements.

But back to the sayings of my mother. (There's a chapter
called 'The Sayings of the Fathers' in the Talmud but I
found my mother's sayings equally educational.)

*The mother of a friend of ours had died. 'Come straight
over, Tommy,' my mother shouted down the telephone.
'I'll pay the taxi.'*

*When Tommy arrived, my practical mother, who had
little time for the dead, said, 'You've got to face facts,
Tommy. What's it going to be – a burial or a cremation?'*

'A cremation, Hetty,' whispered Tommy.

*'Absolutely right,' said my mother and then added,
'I'd make a curry out of the lot of them.'*

*Poor Tommy couldn't believe his ears but I could.
'She means there's enough curry for the lot of us,' I
interposed quickly.*

*Tommy was almost convinced but he gave Ma some
pretty odd looks! And I don't blame him.*

I got some shocks myself even in my mother's very old age.

Coming down the stairs I heard her on the phone. 'Oh,
he died on Monday and the funeral's on Wednesday,'
said my mother sadly. I gathered that an old boyfriend of
hers had died and his son was informing my mother.

She suddenly switched into different mode. 'And now
what's news?' she said cosily. How his mouth must have
dropped at the other end of the line.

In Rome, my mother thought they should turn the Pantheon
into a housing association and so she told a Vatican mon-
signor, who was showing us around his beloved city.
Sometimes she was very clever. In Pisa the guide said, 'This
cathedral was built in the year one thousand.' 'Ah,' said my
mother sagely, gazing at a gargoyle, 'prehistoric animals!'
She did't have much feeling for the past because she was
so engrossed in the present.

'Hetty,' said my mother's high class friend in the coach,
gazing mournfully through the window. 'They're
absolutely ruining the countryside.'

'Oh no,' said my mother brightly, 'look, they're
putting up new tower blocks everywhere!'

Many old people make surprising connections, just like my
mother.

When Pope Julius XI arrived back in Rome from the war,
Michelangelo proudly exhibited to him the wonderful
painted ceiling of the Sistine Chapel. 'Sure, Mike,' said

62

His Holiness, 'you've done a great job, but y'know – I can't help wondering if a nice coat of soft magnolia might be more user-friendly like!'

Another old lady was being shown the same ceiling by a guide. 'It took Michelangelo seven years to finish this ceiling,' said the guide grandly. 'My landlord was like that too,' sighed the lady in agreement.

I never really understood my mother's thinking. She wasn't religious but in her last years she lit candles for her mother, sister and great aunt – never for men. She liked men but thought them irresponsible, which is why she didn't trust God either.

I didn't understood what she thought about me either, though she loved me dearly and would have sacrificed her life for me. While having a curry together, she suddenly said to me, 'Lionel, I'm so pleased you won't have children. They can cause you such pain and anxiety. Believe me, I know.' My jaw dropped. I was her only child. Did she realise what she was saying? I still can't decide. She just carried on munching her Vindaloo.

After the funeral was over and the mourners had left, only the deceased's widow was left sobbing, refusing to forsake the grave.

A stranger suddenly darted out from behind the tombstones and addressed her. 'I love you,' he said passionately, 'I want to marry you.' 'How can you say such things while my husband's coffin is beneath us,' she cried.' 'I must,' he continued, 'because you're so beautiful.' The widow suddenly smiled through her tears and dimpled at him. 'Mister,' she said coyly, 'if only you could see me when my tears don't mess up my maquillage!'

Fathers

There are not nearly as many anecdotes about Jewish fathers as there are about Jewish mothers. They were St Joseph provider figures. They reigned (liturgically at least) but did not rule. Jewish life was matriarchal with patriarchal trappings.

Little Alfie's mother gives him a fillet steak to increase his strength and stamina. But Alfie, who is a sensitive child, bursts into tears. 'I can't help thinking what that poor ox has to go through so that I can have this little steak,' he sobs.

'Don't talk about your father that way!' says his mother, rebuking him sharply.

The Very Old

In old age, after three score years and ten, the minuses are well known. You're like an old car going for its yearly check. Bits and pieces of you go wrong, especially in your waterworks, which may not be the worst but are certainly the most damaging to your dignity. Your memory begins to fade and so does your attention. For some, old age is true tragedy when they feel like young people locked in old people's bodies. They have not bothered to grow up as they grew old. For me, the worst is burying old friends. They can never be replaced.

Before she died, my mother taught me to count my blessings and to make a treat even out of old age. When you're old, she pointed out, you could at last say what you liked and eat what you liked (she liked steak and chips for breakfast and kippers with marmalade). She liked seeing two Zimmers clash, and young couples courting (and more) and life bursting out in all its forms. She taught me not to be envious or jealous.

My great therapy is work. Old people no longer have to doze in corners or be exported to Benidorm. They are also permitted to fall in love and make love – with more foreplay and less climax of course, which is easier on the nerves. They can crack jokes about it. It can be a good time if you know how to handle it and get some support. The old can make and enjoy jokes about their condition, which means they remain on top of it.

A social worker, hurrying to yet another case meeting, sees a 'case' sitting in front of her on a park bench. An old man is sobbing his heart out.

'Is your home a wreck and ruin,' she asks compassionately, 'and you don't want to go back there? Don't worry I'll come with you.'

'Oh no,' he says, 'I've a lovely, warm comfortable house.'

'But perhaps your wife died and you feel alone in it and no one cares for you.'

'Oh no, I married a beautiful young woman immediately after.'

'Oh, I see,' says the social worker. 'You're too old for her and feel inadequate and she's only after your money.'

'No, no it's not like that. She loves old men like me.'

'So what's your problem?' asks the bewildered social worker. 'Look, I'll take you back in my little car and then you won't have to worry about buses or trains,' said the social worker kindly. 'That will be nice, won't it?'

The old man sobs even more. 'You can't,' he cries, 'I've forgotten where I live!'

The mayor enters the old-age home, mortified because there is no red carpet and no one to greet him formally. Angrily he grabs a bent old man passing by on his Zimmer. 'Don't you know who I am?' he shouts.

'Don't be ashamed,' says the old man, adjusting his hearing aid. 'It can happen to any one of us, mate. Just go to that nurse over there. She's got our list. She'll tell you.'

The old man is knocked down by a bus. A nurse rushes over to him and puts a pillow beneath him while waiting for the ambulance. 'Are you comfortable, Mr Cohen?' she enquires. 'I get a living nurse, I get a living,' he replies proudly. A well-meaning priest also rushes over to him, wondering whether to administer the last rites.

'*Do you believe in the Father, Son and Holy Ghost,*' he asks urgently. '*I'm dying so why does he ask me riddles!*' exclaims the perplexed old man to the surrounding crowd.

'*Aren't you worried about your husband going to Ibiza on business without you? How can you let him loose among all those sexy Scandinavian man-eaters?*'

'*Do you see that dog there, chasing the taxis and barking its head off?*' said her friend placidly. '*So say it catches up with one when it stops for a fare, what's he going to do with it!*'

The London traffic is getting faster and faster and more and more confusing the older you get.

The little old lady was trying to cross the road that goes round Marble Arch in London. She was terrified as she dodged buses, honking taxis and speeding sports cars.

One nearly got her and both she and the car driver went white as sheets after he only just missed her.

'*Look where you're going next time!*' *he shouted at her.*

*She went even paler and trembled uncontrollably. '*Mister,*' she cried piteously, wringing her hands, '*are you really coming round again?*'

5

Theology and Religion

Here are some Bible stories you may not have heard before...

The Problems of Israel

I can still laugh, though it's getting harder. But where there's laughter there's hope.

> *This is the root of all Israel's problems:*
>
> *When God allocated lands and territories to all the peoples of the earth, he eventually came to Moses. 'Now what do you want?' he enquired kindly.*
>
> *And Moses said stammeringly (he was slow of speech – the Bible says so) 'Ca-ca-ca-ca-ca...'*
>
> *'Oh, Canaan,' said God. 'Well there's no competition for that. You can have it. I promise it to you. You can call it your Promised Land,' said God magnanimously and sniggered. (Lots of people were promised it but no one has got it.)*
>
> *But what Moses was trying to say was 'California', which was quite a different thing, and that's how the whole mess started.*

The guide shows his tourists the monument to Israel's Unknown Soldier. One of them suspiciously peers at the monument and reads out the plaque. 'To Israel Levy, Israel's Unknown Soldier.' 'How can he be unknown,' he demanded, 'when his name's engraved right there?' 'It's like this,' explained the guide, 'in civilian life, Israel Levy was a well known and respected tailor, I've had a suit from him myself, but as a soldier, between you and me, no one had ever heard of him – he was completely and utterly unknown.'

The trainee Israeli spy is told to take the flight from London to Tel Aviv, proceed to a certain address there and make contact with Cohen, his superior, in utmost secrecy. He should identify himself by saying 'The vultures are roosting.' The young spy arrives in Tel Aviv, saunters with seeming nonchalance to a block of flats and there presses the bell marked 'Cohen'.

An old man opens the door and the trainee croaks in a low voice, 'The vultures are roosting.' The old man looks puzzled and asks him to repeat this information, which the trainee whispers into his ear again. The old man still looks puzzled but suddenly he smiles kindly. 'You've got the wrong Cohen,' he says. 'I'm Cohen the tailor. You want Cohen the spy. He's on the second floor left. The door with peepholes and a double alarm,' he adds helpfully.

'How do you become a millionaire in Israel?' asked the eager and hopeful new Russian immigrant to Israel.

'Come in with a billion!' says the old immigration official cynically.

In the synagogue, whenever the name of Moses was mentioned, everyone in the congregation stood up and cheered in gratitude towards the scrolls. Everyone that is except Mr Cohen. A visitor is struck by his strange attitude and after the service is over asks him the reason for such behaviour. 'If that old fool hadn't gone gaga,' said Mr Cohen through clenched lips, 'and had turned right not left after he crossed the Red Sea, we'd be swimming in oil by now not in all that useless milk and honey.'

Scriptures

You need a firm belief to joke at your own Scriptures. Not many have it. A century of biblical criticism has undermined the old literal belief in them and many have not yet found another way of understanding them.

Are there jokes in the Scriptures? Not easy to say. Trying to understand or even spot the humour of another age, another world, is difficult. There is a thread of laughter running through the Joseph story and I think the last sentence of the Book of Jonah is said by God with, as it were, His tongue in His cheek. And the story of why Sarah named her son 'Laughter' (a form of Isaac in Hebrew) is funny. When I first read it in the original, I actually burst into laughter, disconcerting my erudite university teacher.

I agree that these examples of biblical humour are pretty thin but I have included them for instruction if not for laughs. In the Scriptures God can be heavy going, like his creatures in fact. He is passionate, jealous, angry or loving but he does not smile or laugh much, if at all.

The Birth of Isaac
(Genesis Chapter 21, verses 5-7)

And Abraham was a hundred years old, when his son Isaac was born unto him. And Sarah said, God hath made me to laugh, so that all that hear will laugh with me. And she said, Who would have said unto Abraham, that Sarah should have given children suck? for I have born him a son in his old age.

There is more laughter than at first sight appears. Sarah was pretty ancient too and the rabbis commented that she laughed till her belly shook when she was told she was pregnant. It was all so improbable! That's why she called the child 'Isaac', which means laughter.

The End of the Book of Jonah
(Jonah Chapter 4, verses 9-11)

And God said to Jonah, Doest thou well to be angry for the gourd? And he said, I do well to be angry, even unto death.

> *Then said the Lord, Thou hast had pity on the gourd,*
> *for which thou hast not laboured, neither madest it*
> *grow; which came up in a night, and perished in a night:*
> *And should not I spare Nineveh, that great city, wherein*
> *are more than six-score thousand persons that cannot*
> *discern between their right hand and their left hand;*
> and also much cattle?

It is those last throwaway words – I've put them in roman – which are the giveaway to God's irony with the sulky prophet.

But I think the first identifiable jokes came with the rabbis. There are real jokes in the Talmud, the liturgy they composed and in their sermons. I came across two examples early on in my rabbinical studies. My teacher chose Pesachim (about Passover) as the first tractate of that extraordinary compendium called the Talmud (a collection, a summary and a muddle of rabbinical discussions, which lasted from about the time of Jesus to after 500 AD (CE according to Jewish dating)) that I was permitted to be let loose on. One passage in the tractate particularly puzzled me and he told me I should not take it too seriously because it was only the rabbis making fun of their own expertise and scholasticism. I gaped because the venerable figures I knew seemed very far from such a vulgar concept as 'fun'.

Here is the passage in the Passover tractate. It concerns the duty of ridding your house of all yeast, for example a loaf of bread or indeed any bread, before the festival begins. It is in the name of Rava, a talmudic teacher of the 4th century who lived in Babylon and was noted for his powers of logic and analysis. I am pleased both ran riot in this passage. If you have the Sherlock Holmes spirit, on you go! The original is written in the legal compressed shorthand of early mediaeval Aramaic. I have tried to uncompress it to make it comprehensible. It is something to sort out in a departure lounge of an airport or while waiting for a train. It reminds the secular part of me of the old song 'There was an old man who swallowed a fly. I don't know why he swallowed a fly...'.

> *Rava asked the following question: 'What about the case of a mouse who goes into a house with a piece of bread in its mouth and then a mouse goes out of the house with a piece of bread in its mouth? If you presume that the mouse who went out is the same one who went in then the house is leaven free.*
>
> *But what about the case of a white mouse who went into a house with a piece of bread in its mouth and a black mouse who went out of that house with a piece of bread in its mouth? Surely they must be different mice? But there could be another explanation. Perhaps the black mouse snatched the piece of bread from the white mouse.*
>
> *You might point out that mice don't snatch pieces of bread from each other. In that case what about the following situation when a mouse goes into a house with a piece of bread in its mouth and a weasel (not a mouse) goes out of the house with a piece of bread in its mouth. Is the house leaven free then?*
>
> *Now weasels do indeed snatch pieces of bread from mice but it still might not be the same piece because if it had snatched the piece of bread from the mouse, the mouse would now be in the weasel's mouth as well. (Good point!)*

Alright, you agree that this might be so — then what about the case of a mouse which goes into a house with a piece of bread in its mouth and then a weasel comes out of the house with a piece of bread and also a mouse in its mouth?

This is the same as the case already cited. Or is it? If the case was the same, wouldn't the piece of bread be in the mouse's mouth and the mouse in the weasel's mouth?

Perhaps the piece fell out of the mouse's mouth because of its fright on being taken by the weasel?

The question was not resolved!!! (I give up too!)

In the Passover liturgy the rabbis inflate the number of punishments inflicted on Pharoah into the hundreds by the uses of scholastic methodology. It was a game with the official liturgy in my family to see how we could inflate that number even more, using the same rabbinic methodology. If you were very adept and very learned you could even get into the thousands. I suppose it's no different from the Christian schools in the later Middle Ages having scholastic fun arguing as to how many angels could stand on a pinhead.

If you find this subject moreish, then consult the writings of my fellow lecturer Chaim Maccoby.

Now here is less erudite fare, and I don't blame you for giving a sigh of relief! Here are some stories that clustered around the Old Testament and the New Testament as subversive commentaries, laughing not at God or His emissaries but at the human beings like us that He has to deal with.

What really happened when Jesus met the woman taken in adultery!

Jesus said, 'Let the one who is without sin throw the first stone!'

For a moment nothing happened and then a brick came flying through the air, knocking the woman taken in adultery flat.

'Mother,' said Jesus reproachfully, 'you promised you would stay at home.'

Here's another retelling of the incident in the Gospels when the woman who was possessed by seven devils came to Jesus to cure her. But just as he was about to heal her and expel her devils, she whispered urgently, 'Master, may I have a word with you, may I make a special request?'

'Of course,' he said, 'tell me!'

'Can I tell it to you privately?' she asked furtively.

'Of course,' he said again and bent down, putting his ear close to her mouth.

She whispered into it softly, 'For the present only six and a half please, Master!'

The three wise men come to visit the baby Jesus in the manger, bearing gifts of gold, frankincense and myrrh as the Gospels say. The wise men are very tall but the lintel is very low. The first, bearing gold, bends down and makes it. So does the second, bearing frankincense. But the third, bearing myrrh, doesn't bend low enough and cracks his head on the lintel. 'Jesus Christ!' he exclaims *in agony. Mary turns to Joseph and remarks, 'Now that's a nice name. I was going to call Him Fred!'*

It is said that only when the first man jumped into the Red Sea did the waters part for the children of Israel. And there is great discussion about the identity of that unknown hero. But there is another version. When the Children of Israel got to the Red Sea nobody knew what to do. Someone said to another, 'You go in first,' and the other replied, 'After you,' and then they all began to push and shove till one of them fell into the Red Sea. And that's when the waters opened!

Hell (A Scottish Perspective)

God peered down the black hole to hell to get a better view of His sinners and listened grimly to their shouts.

'Lord, Lord, I couldna ken, I didna ken,' came an anguished cry from below.

'Well, ye ken the nu, ye ken the nu,' retorted God tartly.

A despairing man climbed over a Clyde bridge in Glasgow and stood poised, about to jump in.

'Don't do that!' shouted a passer-by, 'Think of your mother!'

'Haven't got one – she's dead.'
'Then think of your bairns!'
'Haven't got any.'
'Then think of Rangers!'
'I don't support them.'
'Then think of Celtic!'
'I don't support them either.'
'Then jump, yer damned atheist!'
(Rangers was traditionally Glasgow's Protestant team and Celtic its Catholic team.)

The Devil

Does the devil exist? I only know that I sometimes make devils out of perfectly pleasant people who just happen to stand in my way. It's like road rage. Quite often we direct it at the tiresome shopper counting out pennies in front of us at the supermarket queue. Quite often I mentally accuse them of doing to me what I would like to do to them. I sometimes think the devil is just the part of me I don't love. It's worth remembering, though it's very difficult to accept, that all that happens to us, good and bad, can only have one source – God! Simone Weil, one of the greatest spiritual writers of our time, is worth consulting on this subject. I think this is the first time she has ever been recommended in a joke book!

At the church service the visitor was surprised at the behaviour of a little old woman. Every time the devil's name was mentioned, she bobbed her head. Was she a devil worshipper? Surely it could not be a mark of respect? He went up to her and enquired about her strange custom.

'Well,' she said, 'from what I've been told he's a very handsome, charming gent. And at my age, sir, it's best to be prudent. After all, you never know.'

The tempter tried to make a bargain with this chap. 'I'll exchange the whole world with all its riches, its powers and its pleasures in return for your spotted soul,' he offered.

'Hmm, what's the catch?'

Did you hear about the dyslexic devil worshipper who prayed to Santa?

The Messiah

The idea of a Messiah is one of the most potent and disturbing ideas Judaism ever gave to the world. I do not wonder that there are many rabbinic stories trying to discipline and limit it.

A traveller approaching a Jewish village in Eastern Europe comes across a wooden look-out tower just where the road to the village branches off. On the tower sits a man, placidly staring into space. The traveller gets *into conversation with him and enquires what he is on guard against. 'Oh, I'm not guarding against anything,' says the man. 'The village pays me to watch out for the Messiah, so that I can notify them when he comes. Then they can wash and dress properly and prepare themselves to greet him and welcome him fittingly.'*

'How much do they pay you for keeping watch?' asks the curious traveller and exclaims at the smallness of the sum. 'I know it's not much,' said the man, 'but at least it's a steady job.'

Most rabbis did not expect any drastic change in nature (including our own nature) when the Messiah came. For many, like Maimonides the great Jewish philosopher, it would only mean a more just and peaceful world and the return from the exile. So what was to be made of such prophecies as 'The lion shall lie down with the lamb'?

Some thought it meant that wherever a lion and lamb were put together people would have the common sense to put a strong fence between them. Others said, in jest, that the lamb would have to be renewed daily.

Heaven

When I was a congregational rabbi, my congregants kindly brought me back bottles of banana liqueur and videos of their holiday in the Canaries. The former I enjoyed, poured over ice cream. The latter I dreaded. So if Heaven is like an everlasting lecture in paradise, as some rabbis thought, then Hell must be watching the video of it. This old tale seems to me to set the matter straight. My grandpa, who was quite learned in patches, told it to me.

> *A man wanted to see heaven very much and his wish was granted. When he got there he saw the sages poring over their scriptures.*
>
> *'Why,' he said disappointed, 'it's not different from what they were doing on earth.'*
>
> *But God said, 'You've got it the wrong way round. Don't you realise the sages are not in heaven. Heaven is in the sages!'*

And very right too, but our more primitive ideas of heaven take over.

> *The archangel sits at the gate to heaven. A man comes up, starving and emaciated. 'Don't say a word,' says the archangel. 'You are an ascetic for the love of God, it's obvious. Go to Gate 7 for the seventh heaven!'*
>
> *Another man comes up, with open wounds and dripping blood. 'Don't say a word,' says the archangel. 'You are obviously a martyr for the love of God. Go to Gate 7 for the seventh heaven as well!'*
>
> *Mrs Cohen comes up. 'I've organised tombolas for the synagogue,' she says firmly, 'and fashion shows and bridge drives for charity and dances and banquets to raise funds.'*
>
> *'We know all that,' says the archangel politely. 'Go to Gate 2.'*
>
> *'Not Gate 7 for the seventh heaven?' said Mrs Cohen, affronted and alarmed.*

'We thought you might like to have your hair set first,' said the archangel reassuringly.

A man approaches St Peter's desk at the gate of heaven. 'Can I come in?' he asks.

'I don't see why not,' says St Peter, 'but first you have to spell a simple word.'

'What sort of simple word?' says the man suspiciously.

'What about GOD?' says St Peter.

'That's no problem,' says the man, relieved, 'G-O-D.'

'In you come then,' says St Peter kindly, 'and would you mind looking after my desk a moment while I go and talk with Him.'

'Sure,' says the man. He makes himself comfortable and then sees, to his displeasure, his earthly wife approaching.

'How wonderful to see you,' she says. 'Now we can be together for eternity. I missed you so much I drank a bottle of gin and wrapped our car round a tree. Aren't you going to let me in?'

'No problem,' he replies brightly, 'but first you've got to spell a simple word. That's the custom here.'

'What sort of word?' she enquires suspiciously.

'Well, what about Czechoslovakia!'

The young rabbi dies and ascends to heaven. 'We've been expecting you,' said the angels kindly. 'Now what *can we do for you?' 'The only thing I want is to meet my teacher, the holy Rabbi So-and-so.' 'Sure,' said the angels and a door opened up. The young rabbi gave a cry of delight. There was his teacher, the venerable and holy Rabbi So-and-so – but to the young rabbi's amazement a blonde was bouncing up and down on each knee. 'Master,' said his shocked pupil, 'are they the reward of all your piety on earth?' 'My reward? Of course not!' said his former teacher resignedly, 'I'm their punishment!'*

Heaven was often regarded as a party but parties are problems when some of your guests are punctilious about their religious food laws.

A saintly rabbi dies and goes to heaven. 'Wonderful you're here,' say the ministering angels. 'The feast stored up for the righteous is ready for you.'

'That's nice,' said the saint politely, 'but which rabbi supervises the food laws up here?'

'But this is heaven,' explain the bewildered ministering angels.

'It doesn't matter where it is, which rabbi supervises the food laws up here?' he snaps.

'The Holy One, blessed be He Himself, He supervises the food laws,' assert the angels.

The sage considers. 'In that case,' he said cautiously, 'I might risk a cup of tea.'

Theology and Religion

Spiritual Dilemmas and Conundrums

A man falls over the edge of a precipice. Hurtling down he manages to grasp the bough of a small tree growing out from the side of the cliff. Though not normally a religious man, he prays to God nevertheless. 'Put Thy hand out to help me,' he shouts. To his amazement an answering Voice comes from above. 'I shall put out My hand to help thee. I shall hold thee securely. Just let go and trust in Me.' The man is silent, overwhelmed by the Voice and its message.

Then he prays again. In a small voice he whispers, 'Is there anyone else up there?'

Well, there isn't. You either take it or leave it. And if the man leaves it I don't blame him one bit. Religious though I am and a believer, I might very well have said the same!

A man in search of the great teacher and guru is directed to a peak in the Himalayas. When he gets there after terrible hardships, he finds the guru sitting immobile on a frozen rock. 'You may ask three questions,' said the teacher crossly, 'before I return to my meditation.' 'What is this life?' asked the man eagerly.

'Pain and suffering, pain and suffering!' moaned the guru. 'Second question please.' 'But what is beyond this life?' asked the man eagerly.

'More pain, more suffering,' moaned the guru. 'Third and last question please!'

The man cogitated hard. 'Is there another guru higher up?' he whispered.

I do not know what the guru said but I think the answer is 'probably not'. Religion isn't about happiness (this only comes as a by-product) but enlightenment and growth. Hard isn't it? But at least it's not kitsch! But here's a lighter conundrum.

A hospitable congregant invites the rabbi to dinner after the service. The rabbi is shocked. 'How can you?' he said, 'today is the Fast of Zerubavel.' (A minor figure mentioned in the minor prophets. His fast is also minor.) 'Look, rabbi,' said the congregant, 'firstly, even if the Babylonians hadn't killed him, he'd certainly be dead by now. Secondly, if I died would Zerubavel fast for me? Thirdly, I don't even keep a major fast like the Day of Atonement so why should I fast on a minor one like this?'

Here's a clerical conundrum!

For the funeral eulogy a rabbi must be honest but he must also be complimentary. In this case the task seemed impossible. The dead man had led a life of unredeemed villainy and selfishness. 'What shall I do?' he asked an older rabbi. 'What can I say?'

'Don't worry,' said the old man. 'Just trust in God and He will help you. He will put the right words into your mouth.'

The interment took place and the rabbi started the sermon by the grave.

'He wasn't exactly a popular man,' he said hesitantly. 'His wife isn't here because she left him long ago, not

able to stand it any more. And his children aren't here because they're on the streets because he was such a bad father to them. And there are no friends here – at least not personal ones – because he didn't have any.'

The rabbi paused, uncertain how to continue. Then an amazed smile came over his face. God had come to his aid as the older rabbi said he would. 'But,' he continued confidently, 'compared to his big brother, this man was a saint!'

Food

Jewish jokes on food are innumerable. If you're not Jewish and want to enjoy the humour, you had better research the food laws fast. As much theology is imbibed through the mouth as through the mind.

> A man wearing the traditional skull cap goes into a delicatessen. He inspects what's on offer and after lingering a long time in thought points to his choice and says to the attendant, 'I'll have a pound of that smoked salmon there.'
> 'That's not smoked salmon, sir,' sings out the attendant helpfully, 'that's smoked ham.'
> 'Do other customers ever compliment you on your big mouth,' whispers the old man softly.

> An Italian mother shouts out, 'If you don't finish my spaghetti, I'll kill you.'
> But a Jewish mother just whispers, 'If you don't finish my chicken soup, I'll kill myself!'
> I think the Jewish mother wins!

> Abie, though a bootlegger in New York in the twenties, still kept the old pieties and every Friday night visited his

dear old mother for the Sabbath. But one Sabbath a rival gang lay in wait for him and as he knocked on his mother's door, they sprayed him with bullets. As he slipped down the door, dripping blood, she opened it.

'Ma,' he said, 'they've got me.'

'Quiet!' she said, 'soup first. We can talk later.'

Mrs Goldberg inspects a chicken, the classical Jewish festival food, at the butcher's. She prods the bird's breast, eyes it for colour and then opens its legs and thrusts her nose between them to smell it better.

'It doesn't smell fresh to me,' she says to the butcher accusingly.

'Madam,' said the butcher, 'would you smell any different if I did the same to you!'

My mother would do anything for her boss, who was vegetarian and too fastidious to eat in a normal restaurant. However, she was not good at cooking or machines but he didn't realise this and presented her with a machine to juice vegetables for his lunch.

Well, Ma thought the carrots weren't going round fast enough so she managed to stick her finger in to encourage them. How she did it I don't know, because it was impossible, but when she decided on something she didn't allow details to stop her.

Covering her mutilated member with a napkin, she managed to serve the juice and make it back to her office kitchen before she fainted.

When she came to for a few minutes in hospital, she whispered, 'Thank God it was carrots not spinach...the colour...so lucky!' She then passed out again.

All this happened long, long ago when jobs were hard to come by. I don't think her boss, sipping my mother's life blood, ever realised what a potent non-kosher brew he was drinking.

At the Restaurant

I used to work as a waiter during the university vacation but I was too weakened by religion to be tough enough. In a Jewish restaurant you didn't tell the waiters what you wanted to eat, they told you. And to get your food you had to butter them up! It was a university of life. In many old style restaurants they're still like that but there's been a customer revolt in recent years brought on by the fawning ways of non-kosher starred eateries.

The customer waited and waited but his order didn't arrive.

Angrily he called the manager over and complained about the delay in the service.

'Is this one of those hoity-toity, anti-Semitic eateries?' he demanded fiercely, preparing his fists for action.

The manager looked around quickly and then whispered into his ear, 'Between ourselves, sir, have you ever tasted our food?'

Food

Morry waited patiently during the long delay between his order and its arrival.

'Are you the same waiter I gave my order to?' he asked politely.

'Are you nuts or something,' said the waiter suspiciously, 'Sure I'm the same waiter, don't you recognise me?'

'I was beginning to expect a far older man,' said the diner deprecatingly.

The diner orders some soup and the waiter brings a bowl of it. The diner doesn't bother to taste it. 'Take it back,' he says 'and make it hotter.' The waiter takes the soup away and brings some more. The diner looks at it and then demands again that it be reheated and brought back. The furious waiter does so and the diner says, 'That's fine now, just how I like it.'

The waiter explodes, 'How can you say it wasn't hot enough when you didn't even taste any of it?'

'This time,' said the diner tucking in, 'you didn't have your thumb in it!'

The customer shouts, 'The service in this restaurant is frightful!'

One waiter to another, 'He's a fool! How can he tell, when he never gets any!'

The customer, angrily, 'There's something wrong with this fish. It smells funny.'
   The tired waiter, 'So laugh!'

Sometimes the drama wasn't provided by the waiters but by the customers.

A Jewish gentleman sees a Chinese gentleman in the restaurant and for some reason this incites his ire. Perhaps his wife had just left him for ever, or had just left him for ever and returned, or perhaps he had just left her for ever but she didn't even notice – who can say? Anyway, he picked up a plate of chicken noodle soup and poured it over the Chinese gentleman. 'That's for Pearl Harbour,' he growled.

'But I'm Chinese!' exclaimed the gentleman indignantly, 'not Japanese.'

'Chinese, Japanese, Siamese – who cares,' said the morose Jew. It's all the same to me. What's in a name?'

As the Jewish gentleman got up to pay his bill, the Chinese guy hit him over the head with a salami. 'That,' he said, 'is for the sinking of the Titanic.' 'But the Titanic was sunk by an iceberg,' said the Jewish gentleman indignantly.

'Goldberg, Rosenberg, Greenberg, Iceberg – what's in a name!'

Food

The waiter's attention is riveted by one of his customers who appears to be talking to the boiled fish he ordered.

'What's he telling you?' says the waiter, his curiosity overcoming his disbelief.

The man bends down again and whispers at the fish's head. 'He's trying to tell me the story of his life,' says the man. 'How he lived in the Mediterranean till he was caught – that sort of thing.'

'Ask him what life was like there?' asks the waiter fascinated.

Again the man leans down, whispers to the fish and listens.

'He says you must excuse him. It was all so long ago, so much time has passed since he came out of the water, that he can hardly remember anything about it any more, poor fish.'

Sometimes, of course, the waiter took a liking to you and let you in on some much needed information. Waiters could be your cynical therapists.

Now Morry had been battered, economically and emotionally. Needing some comfort food he sat down in the restaurant looking glum.

'What's your order?' said the waiter dispassionately.

'Fish balls like my mother used to make,' said Morry. 'And a kind word,' he begged.

The waiter snickered and shrugged his shoulders and a few minutes later returned with the fish balls.

'And what about my kind word?' implored Morry, as the waiter left the table.

The waiter looked at him for a moment and then whispered into his ear, 'If I were you, I wouldn't touch the fish.'

Sometimes the diners took a liking to their waiter as well.

One sighed and muttered to himself as he was tucking in his napkin, 'If only old Abie was still alive and serving us. Dinner doesn't taste like dinner without him.'

Suddenly his flesh begins to shake because a see-through Abie is standing in front of him, picking his teeth with a toothpick, as was his wont. The diner gets nervous indigestion and bolts, his borscht hardly touched.

Speaking of this with his fellow diners they decide to organise a séance to actually speak to Abie and ask where he is and what the food's like there. They hire a medium and sit round a comfortable table. And nothing happens! 'You must have been seeing things or drunk too much,' say the others.

The next day the diner sees see-through Abie again, shimmering by the salt beef. 'Why did you do the dirty on me, Abie, and make a laughing stock out of me. It wasn't nice, Abie. I had some bets on you too.'

'What could I do,' said Abie, 'if you don't choose one of my tables!'

7

Holidays and Vacations

Putting On the Style –
When We Live a Little Bit Above Ourselves

An English couple at a famous Paris restaurant. The husband examines his salad and then calls the waiter over and points to a black spot in it. 'La mouche!' he says courteously, showing off his French. 'Le mouche,' corrects the waiter haughtily.

'Good God,' says the Englishman, polishing his spectacles, 'My! What wonderful eyesight you've got!'

An elderly, nouveau riche couple hire a yacht. The husband falls off it and is rescued by a sailor. 'Artificial respiration!' shouts the sailor urgently. 'Real respiration or nothing!' shouts back his wife, determinedly barring the way.

At the captain's table a guest admires her neighbour's diamond ring. 'Yes, it's the famous Goldberg diamond,' says the owner wearily. 'But it's got a real curse on it,' she adds sombrely.

The guest is thrilled. 'Tell me about the curse,' she says eagerly.

'It is coming ever nearer and nearer,' intoned the other. 'Ever closer, ever closer! It's almost upon us,' she whispered fearfully. 'Why,' she says brightly, 'here is my husband, Mr Goldberg himself. Let me introduce you!'

There is a fearful crash on the approach road to the airport. A sleek car suffers the greatest damage. The police calm the driver through a shattered window, telling him not to worry, they will soon get him out by cutting through the chassis. 'Oh, my Rolls, Oh, my Rolls,' he moans.

The doctor arrives, examines him and tells him to be courageous because they will have to amputate his arm as well. 'Oh, my Rolex, Oh, my Rolex,' moans the stricken man!

Mrs Goldberg left instructions in her will that her ashes be scattered along Bond Street. 'Then,' she said, 'I'll be certain my daughter-in-law will visit me at least twice a week.'

Fantasy and Reality

On holiday our fantasy meets our reality. Reality always catches up with us. We should remember that perfection is not possible in this world, only in another dimension.

One of the most difficult things is keeping your business preoccupations away from your holiday – being able to switch off. These two businessmen didn't succeed. They were on a safari holiday journeying through a swamp when a slimy leathery reptile wound itself round the foot of one of them.

'My God, what's that?' he screamed.

'Don't ask me,' shouted the other, 'you're the one who sells leather lingerie!'

Two men are discussing their hotels in the departure lounge.

'Ours was a lovely hotel,' said the first, 'it was in an undiscovered, most beautiful part of Provence. And there was the wonderful simple home cooking. When the calf died we had a magnificent Blanquette de Veau, and when the cow died a Boeuf Bourguignon I shall never forget. And what a Poulet Henri IV after the chicken disappeared.'

'How long did you stay there?' said the other.

'Well,' said the first hesitantly, 'not right to the end of our holiday. You see the patron died while we were there and we thought perhaps we would go self-catering!'

As we get older the men disappear faster than the women and so it becomes harder and harder for an older woman to find a partner. *C'est la vie*!

At the Lloret Hotel the lady spies a man on the beach, big muscled and pale.

'Haven't seen you round here before mister,' she says conversationally. 'Where've you been? You look kinda pale, mister. Shall I smear you with sun oil?' she offers hopefully.

'I've been in caboose, in jail,' he grunts.

'How long were you in this caboose, this jail, mister,' she enquires delicately, anointing his shaven bumpy scalp.

'Fifteen years,' he grunts again.

'Would you like one of my famous facials?' she says cosily. And casually adds, 'Why did they put you in this caboose?'

'Because I strangled my wife,' he sneered.

'Oh, mister,' she says, slapping him coyly with her fan, 'you should have told me you were single!'

A lady introduces a newcomer to the hotel at the bridge table.

'I'm Mrs Colqehoun,' she says, 'and this is Mrs Carstairs and this is Mrs de Cartier.'

'So nice to meet you, ladies,' says the newcomer comfortably. 'So nice to meet up with other Cohens.'

A lady books a beach holiday in a modern hotel by the Black Sea. But the hotel is overbooked and to her dismay she is transferred to a Dracula-inspired mediaeval castle.

In her echoing empty bedroom she shivers as she gets into bed.

She is suddenly awakened in the night by banging. And looking up she screams. A vampire is beating its wings against the bars over the window. They give way and the vampire flies towards her throat on its massive wings.

But the lady in her desperation pulls off the cross she is wearing on a gold chain round her neck and holds it defiantly in front of her.

'Darlink,' said the vampire sympathetically, 'dat von't help. Oy oy oy, dis ain't your lucky day, baby, is it.'

Two holidaymakers on a crowded charter flight, enjoying their duty frees, were disturbed to hear an old man crying in the seat behind them.

'Oy, oy! I'm so unheppy,' he wailed. 'Oy, oy! I'm so unheppy!'

They couldn't stand it. They turned round and did all they could for the old man. They gave him a cushion and a cup of tea and a newspaper and were settling back for another snort of cheap whisky when the crying started all over again with increased vigour.

'Oy, oy, I'm so heppy,' he wailed. 'Oy, oy, I'm so heppy, oy, oy, I'm so heppy!'

A woman sends a holiday postcard to her psychotherapist. It reads, 'I'm so enjoying myself. But why?'

8

Ecumenism

Anglican Wit

The two little boys disliked each other at prep school and again at public school and didn't see each other again till they met at a station decades later on their way to an old boys' reunion. In the meantime one had become a mighty admiral and the other a proud bishop. When the bishop recognised the admiral the devil got into him. 'Stationmaster,' he said loudly, addressing the admiral, 'could you please indicate the platform for London?'

'In your condition, madam,' replied the admiral superciliously, 'I would be inclined to take a taxi.' And he stalked off.

A drunk staggers into a crowded railway carriage, inserts himself next to a disapproving clergyman, and peruses a paper that has been left behind. 'What are arthritis and gout?' he suddenly asks the clergyman. The latter sees a chance to shame the drunk. 'They are,' he says, 'diseases of the flesh, caused by excessive carousing, the punishments for port drinking, womanising and gluttony.'

'Hm, it says here,' says the drunk, pointing at the paper, 'that your Archbishop's got both.'

An agitated worshipper rushes to a cathedral canon and tells him that a woman has just had a vision of God peering down at her from the pulpit. What should she do?

The perplexed canon rushes to the bishop to tell him. 'What should she do?' he asks excitedly.

'Look busy!' says the bishop.

I was told this by an Anglican priest.

When Montgomery Campbell, the newly appointed Bishop of London, came to take possession of his cathedral, his chaplain knocked three times at the great doors, according to custom. But the canons within, being old and deaf, didn't hear. After more vigorous knocking, however, they opened up for their new bishop, who surveyed them indulgently. 'Ah,' he is reported to have said, 'the See bringeth forth its dead!'

At Oxford I knew many Anglican hopefuls and they used to tell me anecdotes about Dean Inge, if I egged them on and bribed them with bits of Jewish food. Apparently he took his pastoral duties very seriously and on Sunday mornings he used to drop in unannounced to the churches of his diocese and listen interestedly to the sermons.

After one morning service, he asked the preacher to see him. 'Excuse me, Mr X,' he is said to have said. 'Perhaps you could tell me how you prepare your sermons.'

'Certainly,' said the Reverend Mr X. 'The first part I work out carefully myself but for the second part I abandon myself to the inspiration of the Holy Ghost.'

'Thank you so much,' answered the Dean. 'I hope you won't think me blasphemous, Mr X, if I tell you that I far prefer your part!'

Roman Catholic Humour

Earthier than the Anglican and not so classy. More like the Jewish sort.

Two labourers are repairing the church roof. One gazes down, sees an old woman praying and they decide to have some fun at her expense. 'Mary Kelly!' one intones. Nothing happens. The other then bellows down, 'Mary Kelly!' Again, nothing happens and the woman continues praying. Annoyed, both boom down together, 'Mary Kelly!' The old woman sighs and looking up says, 'Can't yer be quiet for a minute like, while I'm just having a little chat with yer mother?'

A joke making its way round Rome but not normally printed.

His Holiness is so worried by the future of the Church, he begs God to reassure him.

'You can ask three questions,' says God.

'Will there ever be women priests?'

'Not in your lifetime, John Paul.'

'Will there ever be married clergy?'

'Not in your lifetime, John Paul.'
'Will there ever be another Polish Pope?'
'Not in my lifetime, John Paul.'

A priest and three nuns carrying luggage rush onto the platform and the nuns with the luggage get into a carriage just in time. As they start stowing away the luggage the train pulls out.

The stationmaster rushes over to the priest left behind and apologises because he has just missed his train.

'Oh, don't apologise to me,' said the priest comfortingly. 'I'll just get the next one. I'm thinking about those poor dear sisters who just came with me to see me off.'

Two priests are walking in the park when they hear a cry and they see a man stranded in a tree. 'You're stuck in that tree!' they shout up.

'You must be Dominicans,' the man shouts down.

'That's right, but how do you know?' they answered, amazed.

'Because what you say is absolutely correct and of no damn use to anyone!'

This last story was told me incidentally by a Dominican. It is encouraging when religious people can tell jokes against themselves. Not many can.

Blue's Jokes

Not Getting Uppity – A Lesson in Ecumenism

One of the lessons you learn in an ecumenical age is that no tradition or religion has a monopoly of goodness or wisdom or humour, whatever they taught you to the contrary in religion classes or Sunday school. I used to think, for example, that Jews had a monopoly of humour but when I began to mix with Christians I realised this was not so. It's an important lesson and stops you getting uppity.

Here are some of the jokes I learnt, walking with monks in monasteries or cooking for nuns and priests on retreat.

A burglar breaks into a house while the owners are out. He feels for the safe in the darkness and is just about to break it open when he hears a voice and freezes. 'Jesus is watching you!' says the voice. 'Jesus is watching you!' The burglar flashes his torch to see where the voice is coming from and a sigh of relief goes through his body when he only sees a parrot on a perch. 'What a pretty bird you are,' he says ingratiatingly. 'And what a nice name – I've never met a parrot called Jesus before.'

'My name is Polly,' said the parrot proudly. 'Jesus is the name of our big bull terrier behind you!'

One of the nicest developments of the last 50 years has been the thaw in Christian/Jewish relations. When I was a young minister we sometimes had Christian/Jewish get-togethers. In a cold church hall, the priest said how nice it was that I was a Jew and I batted back by saying how nice it was that he was a Christian. And then we were promptly served with cups of tea lest we say anything dangerous.

But now we can tell each other jokes about each other and not be frightened of showing each other our dirty washing. All of this witnesses to the growth in trust which has taken place among us. Such exchanges would have been inconceivable 40 years ago. Have you heard these? I heard them while peeling potatoes during a retreat.

There was a police raid on a gambling den and three clergymen were arrested. The judge turned first to the priest. 'As you are a man of the cloth, I shall accept your word. Did you gamble?'

'Lord, forgive me,' said the priest under his breath. 'No, your honour, I didn't,' he said aloud.

The judge then addressed the pastor and asked him the same question. 'Pardon me, Lord,' whispered the pastor. 'No your honour, I didn't.'

'Well,' said the judge turning to the rabbi, 'what about you? As a man of the cloth, did you gamble?'

'Me gamble, milord!' said the rabbi, astonished. 'Who would I gamble with?'

A little Jewish boy has a Catholic friend at school. 'Can I visit your church?' he asks curiously. 'Sure,' said the little Catholic boy – you're welcome. But when people go forward to the communion rail, you mustn't go along with them. Just stay behind!' 'Why?' said the little Jewish boy. 'Because you'll become Christian and there'll be nothing you can do about it.' 'Will I?' said the little Jewish boy intrigued.

But during the church service he is so carried away by the candles, the incense, the music and the robes that when everyone streams forward to the communion rail he goes along with them as in a dream.

'I told you not to go to the communion rail,' said his little Catholic friend gloomily. 'You're a Christian now and there's nothing we can do about it.' 'Am I?' said the little Jewish boy overwhelmed. 'Oh yes,' said his friend firmly.

The Jewish boy returned home, slowly pondering the situation. 'Ma,' he says, 'there's something I've got to tell you – it's important.' 'Darling,' said his mother, 'I haven't got time to listen. I've got to make supper before we all go to bingo tonight. Go and tell your father. He's always got time on his hands.'

In the garage the little boy says, 'Dad, I've got something terribly important to tell you.' 'Sonny, I haven't got time,' said his father. 'I've got to fix the car for bingo tonight. Go and speak to your sister. She's only mooning over the telephone.'

'Sis!' says the boy, 'I must speak to you. It's urgent!' 'And so is the call I'm expecting from my boyfriend,' she says. 'Tell me another time.'

The little boy goes and sits on the steps. 'I've only been a Christian for an hour,' he says to himself feelingly, 'and I'm already beginning to dislike Jews!'

The congregant's face is ashen white. 'Rabbi, I don't know how to tell it – it's so dreadful.' 'Take your time,'

said the rabbi gently. 'You know my daughter, the clever one who's gone to study medicine in Cambridge.' The rabbi nods. 'Well, she's met a born-again Christian and she's become a born-again Christian too!' The man sobs with grief.

The rabbi now looks ashen too. 'How terrible that you've come to me,' he said. He swallows hard. 'It's so difficult to tell,' he says, 'but you know my son who's studying economics in Oxford.' His congregant nods. 'Well,' continued the rabbi in a whisper, 'he's met a Catholic girl up there and he's becoming a Catholic too! We can't help each other,' said the rabbi. 'We're in the same situation. Only God can help us!'

They file into the synagogue and the rabbi opens the Ark. Reverently they lay their problems before God.

An anguished voice suddenly comes down from heaven. 'Why ask me?' says the voice, tearfully, 'I had a son ...'

A Jewish convert to Catholicism finds it hard to make the break from the Jewish practices he has kept since childhood, like lighting the Sabbath candles for example. He finally consults the priest who converted him.

'You've got to be firm with yourself,' said the priest. 'On Friday nights, say to yourself again and again, "I'm a Catholic not a Jew, I'm a Catholic not a Jew". It's only habit and that should deal with it.'

Some weeks later, passing by his convert's house on a Friday, he peers through the open window to see how he

*is getting on. His convert is gazing at a plate of Jewish
chicken soup and dumplings with greedy hunger in his
eyes and saying over it, 'You're a piece of fish, not chicken
soup, you're a piece of fish not chicken soup ...'*

Probably converts the other way have the same problems!

Ecumenical Problems of Prayer

The best place to pick up ecumenical jokes is in the
scullery, peeling and scraping potatoes with other clergy.
The tap water cleans away your caution and you end up
telling each other those jokes which give the game away
about your own little lot and are usually only communicated
in whispers to close colleagues. A selection of holy cook-
house jokes! This is a very ancient and therapeutic joke:

*The rabbi is stranded by a flood. He perches on the roof
of his house and prays to God to help him.*

*A rowing boat comes by and offers to evacuate him
but the rabbi dismisses it. 'God Himself will help me,' he
says. 'I trust in Him and wait for His rescue.'*

*A helicopter sees his plight and hovers over him,
ready to pick him up. But the rabbi again waves it away.
'God will be sure to help me,' he says.*

*Night is coming on and the rabbi feels intensely cold.
'Oh God, remember thy servant,' he prays.*

*A swimmer with a spare lifejacket gets near the roof
but again the rabbi tells him not to bother, for God will
be sure to intervene.*

Ecumenism

The night has now come on and the rabbi prays to God again, reminding God how he has always trusted in Him.

This time a weary voice comes from heaven in answer to his prayer. 'I have sent My boat, My plane and My swimmer to do precisely that but you, silly man, sent them all away out of pride. What more can I do?'

Sometimes the means of salvation are so ordinary and so obvious we ignore them. They are not dramatic or individual enough for us. I used to cry to God because I had never met Mr Right who would look after me in life. But looking back on life, I see that all I asked for was there in front of me but it wasn't exotic enough. How could I have been such a fool and too much of a snob to see what was in front of my eyes?

The little boy composes a letter to Jesus before Christmas. 'Dear Jesus,' he writes, 'if I am good for a month, may I please have a computer for Christmas.' He is not satisfied. A month is an awfully long time for a little boy – breakfast, lunch, tea, breakfast, lunch, tea ... It's too much. He throws the letter in his wastepaper basket and starts again.

'Dear Jesus,' he writes, 'if I am good for a week, may I please have a computer for Christmas.' But even this is too much in the life of a little boy and he throws away that letter too.

Then an idea occurs to him. He gently takes down his statue of Our Lady, wraps it in his clean handkerchief, puts it in the drawer of his desk, locks the drawer and puts the key in his pocket.

He then starts yet another letter. 'Dear Jesus,' he writes, 'if you ever want to see your mum again …'

A man going into the church bumps against another man, also going in. 'What are you going in for?' says the first to the second, who replies, 'I'm going in to ask God for a tenner because I'm really down on my luck.' 'A tenner!' exclaims the first. 'Why, I'm going to consult Him about my ten million pound business empire.' He takes out his wallet, peels off a tenner and gives it to the second man. 'Here's your tenner,' he says, 'now be off with you,' and the second man goes away, rejoicing.

The first then enters the church, kneels down in his pew and starts to pray. 'Lord,' he says, 'now that I have your undivided attention …'

Izzie goes into a synagogue. 'Lord,' he says, 'I've never asked you for anything before but may I please have a small win on the lottery because I'm broke. I hearken for your reply, Lord.'

A week later he goes into the synagogue again. 'Lord,' he says, 'I know I'm not very important but I only wanted one small win on the lottery. I hope you haven't forgotten. I wait for your reply, Lord.' Again, no reply comes.

A few days later Izzie tries yet again. 'I suppose,' he prays, aggrieved, 'that I'm not important enough for you to bother about but I only wanted a very small win on the lottery. Couldn't you help me, Lord?'

This time a voice does come down from heaven. 'Izzie, Izzie,' it says, 'couldn't you help me a little too! Couldn't you at least buy one lottery ticket?'

A pious lady was walking beside the sea with her little granddaughter when a great wave crashed over them, sucking the child into the sea. The lady was frantic and ran up and down the beach crying, 'Oh God, give me back my granddaughter, give me back my granddaughter! Suddenly, another wave crashed onto the sand and, battered and bewildered but not really hurt, the little child lay at her feet restored to her.

Her grandmother then ran up and down the beach crying, 'What about the hat I knitted for her? What about her knitted hat?'

More Interfaith Misunderstandings

Many forms of religion are exclusive and introverted. The inclusive thinking of the prophets is rare. This provides a fertile ground for misunderstandings. Believers often think they know the answers before they have even listened to the questions!

That secular Jewess, Gertrude Stein, knew better than many believers. I was told that on her deathbed she drifted back into consciousness and asked, puzzled, 'What is the answer?' She drifted back into unconsciousness again but then tried to sit up and asked, 'But what is the question?' This story may be apocryphal but it is in character. What a perceptive woman!

On the doorpost of a Jewish house or flat there is usually a discreet wooden, metal or plastic case about two-thirds of the way up on the right hand side. If you are not Jewish you may never have noticed it; if you are Jewish you are only too aware of it because besides indicating piety it is also a quick and handy guide for fundraisers for Jewish charities. Inside the little box there is a piece of parchment that contains verses from the Five Books of Moses and the important words are, 'you shall write these words on the doorposts of your house and upon your gates'. The words in question refer to the unity of God and the commandment to love Him. This pietistic device is called a *mezuzah* because *mezuzah* means doorpost in Hebrew. I am sorry the joke requires such a lot of explanation – that's a bad sign with jokes. Never mind, it must be good for your soul and I think the joke is worth it.

Well, this Jewish family moves into their new house and, of course, they fix their mezuzah. *The non-Jewish family next door are curious about it.*

'What's it for?' asked their new neighbour, politely.

'Oh, it contains some words to remember God whenever we go in,' said the Jewish man.

'I see,' said the non-Jewish man, non-committally, but he didn't. He was convinced there was more to it than that. So when the Jewish family went out for supper, he took a

screwdriver and unloosened the nails of the outer case.
Sure enough, there was a piece of parchment inside just as
the Jewish man had said. He opened it up and it read,
'HELP, I'M A PRISONER IN A MEZUZAH FACTORY!'

A more fundamental misunderstanding concerns the
Talmud, the great work of rabbinic Judaişm.

A non-Jew comes to a Jewish rabbi and begs him to
teach him the Talmud. 'It won't help,' said the rabbi,
'non-Jews haven't got the head for such things. You have
to be born with it.'

'Try me, try me!' said the non-Jewish man.

'Very well,' said the rabbi, 'but it won't get you any-
where. Now listen carefully!' The rabbi then chants the
following question – 'If two men come down a chimney
and one comes out sooty and the other comes out clean,
which goes to wash first?'

'The sooty one, of course,' said the student, 'that's
easy.'

'Fool,' said the rabbi. 'Look, the sooty one sees the
clean one and says, if he's clean, then I must be clean
and stays where he is. And the clean one looks at the
sooty one and says, if he's sooty, I must be sooty, so he
rushes off to wash first. I told you,' sighed the rabbi,
'non-Jews haven't got the head for such things.'

'Try me, try me again!' demanded the non-Jew. 'Give
me another question.' The rabbi sighs even deeper and
says, 'Very well, here it is. Listen carefully! If two men
go down a chimney and one comes out sooty and the
other clean, which goes to wash first.'

> *'Oh, I know the answer to that one,' chortles the non-Jew. 'The clean one goes to wash first.'*
>
> *'Fool,' said the rabbi, 'whoever heard of two men coming down a chimney and one coming out sooty and the other clean? Didn't I tell you, you have to be Jewish to have a head for such things!'*

There are many multi-purpose jokes that you can turn any way you like. They are useful in showing up the stupidity of prejudice. This one I first heard from a Northern Irishman against Catholics but not long after I heard it from another Northern Irishman against Protestants. Later on I heard a different form of it told by Israeli nationalists against Arabs and I'm sure Arab nationalists must be telling it against Israelis. It is a very useful joke if you are on a journey through Bosnia, say, or Macedonia, or Kashmir, or the Holy Land, or anywhere. The version I know starts off in a bar (or snug, souk or coffee house).

> *A man enters with his pet crocodile and says to the barman, 'Do you serve Catholics here?' 'Certainly Sir,' said the barman. 'Then one for me and one for my croc,' says the man.*

Substitute Protestant for Catholic where necessary according to your prejudice and preference! There's another on similar lines.

> *A man in Belfast feels a gun in his back. 'Are you a Protestant or a Catholic? says a voice. The man thinks quickly. 'I'm Jewish,' he says. 'But are you a Protestant Jew or a Catholic Jew?' continues the voice urgently.*

And here's another Northern Ireland story for good measure. It's not just anti-Protestant or anti-Catholic but a bit anti-Semitic too.

> *Hymie feels a knife in his back.*
>
> *'Which is it, yer money or your life?' croaks a man with a Belfast whine.*
>
> *Hymie doesn't answer and the man repeats his question angrily.*
>
> *'Give me time, give me time!' says Hymie. 'I've got to think.'*

And this is not quite nasty but sort of comic.

> *A man feels a gun in his back and hears the dreaded words, 'What are yer, Catholic or Protestant?'*
>
> *'I'm neither,' says the man triumphantly. 'I'm Jewish.'*
>
> *'Then ain't I the luckiest Ayrab in Belfast,' comes the response.*

> *An Israeli guy applies to join an extreme nationalist organisation. He is closely examined. 'We want you to assassinate any Palestinian and any parrot fancier you meet. OK?'*
>
> *The Israeli scratches his head. 'Why the parrot fancier?' he asks bewildered.*
>
> *'You're in,' say his examiners!*

Now try to say the same 'joke' with the nationalities reversed! What about Israelis and insurance agents?

113

Christians of course have their misunderstandings. Jews have no monopoly of booboos. I was told a story about the saintly Bishop Bell at a Christian ecumenical conference:

For the first time a western Protestant church had voted together with an Orthodox church and the delegates felt that truly the Holy Ghost had at last hovered over them. The subject was about the Church Visible and the Church Invisible. But Bishop Bell, besides being saintly, was also very astute and curious.

'Who were the Church Visible?' he inquired afterwards of the Protestant church delegates. They not unexpectedly answered that the Church Visible consisted of all their own members. 'And the Church Invisible?' 'All other Christians, not members of our own church,' they answered.

Bishop Bell then went round to the Orthodox delegates and asked them the same question. 'The Church Visible,' they said, 'consists of all living members of the Orthodox church. And the Church Invisible of the same people when dead!'

In religion it is often best not to ask too much. Mohammed rightly answered pedantic enquirers about the Koran that they should desist and thank God for having given them a short scripture.

I myself caused chaos at a preparatory meeting for the German Evangelical Conference, their Kirchentag. The discussion concerned the two Reichs. I was tired from my long journey, German was hard work and I was falling asleep.

Suddenly I heard my name called and was asked to give my special Jewish viewpoint. I have forgotten what I said but it seemed to cause much heart searching among the delegates. But after intense discussion all was revealed. They found out that I had thought they meant the two states into which Germany was divided at that time, the Federal Republic and the DDR. How was I to know that the two Reichs was a key concept of Lutheran theology and signified this world and the next! They were very nice to me after that and even amused but I have never been invited back again.

Modern Times

The Nazis

Jokes about the Nazis are innumerable (and strangely gentle – in jokes they are often pictured as fools rather than sadists).

When the refugees came over to London from the continent, each one had a more dreadful tale to tell about what life was like there. I wanted to listen but for weeks afterwards I got nightmares. I am still grateful to a refugee who wrapped the horror in jokes to protect me from my own anger. Jokes helped me absorb the reports of the Nazi persecutions when I was a child. I got the message but didn't have nightmares afterwards.

A circus is coming to town in Germany during the Nazi times and announces that anyone who will go into a cage with a roaring, hungry, vicious lion would get a hundred marks. Jobs were scarce for Jews so this Yiddish guy decides to volunteer. 'Though I die,' he said to himself, 'at least my wife and child will have a hundred marks to live on.'

So when the circus arrives he volunteers and he is thrust forward to the cage. The door is open and he is pushed in. He is on one side of the cage and the roaring, hungry, vicious lion is on the other. The audience is thrilled!

The Yiddish guy then closes his eyes and says the prayers that are said before death, before martyrdom.

'Hear, O Israel, the Lord is our God, the Lord is One,' he intones.

But then his jaw drops as he hears the lion reply, 'And blessed is His holy name whose kingdom is for ever and ever.'

'Remember, you're not the only Jew in Germany, grandpa, who's trying to earn a living,' continues the lion.

The following 'joke' is blacker than any that Liverpool could come up with.

The concentration camp commandant picks up a little Jewish child. 'One of my eyes is real and the other is artificial. If you can tell me which is the artificial one, I might spare your parents.'

The child carefully examined both eyes. 'That one is real,' she said, pointing. 'How did you guess?' said the amazed commandant. 'Because the other one looked almost human,' she said.

The stormtrooper bumps into a Jew on the pavement.

'Schwein!' shouts the stormtrooper.

'Cohen,' replies the Jew, doffing his hat.

This was one of the blackest ones I've ever heard. It came from Russia from where my grandmother had fled.

A man bursts into a synagogue as the congregation is saying the afternoon prayers.

*'A girl has been found dead in the river,' he shouts,
'What are we going to do?'*

*The congregation trembles because Jews would be
held responsible and soon there would be a riot and a
pogrom would begin.*

*They are about to rush home, gather their few belong-
ings and flee, when another man rushes through the
door. 'Don't worry, don't worry,' he shouted, 'God be
thanked, the murdered girl was Jewish!'*

There are, of course, Jews being Jews, even funny jokes
about pogroms.

*A man bursts into a Jewish home. 'Flee,' he shouts, 'a
pogrom is starting. The mob will pillage our homes and
rape our women. Even the old won't be safe!'*

*'What's going to happen to granny?' asked her grand-
daughter tremulously. 'She can't be moved. I'll stay here
with her.'*

*'Go off all of you!' said the granny. 'You owe it to your
children but I'm going to stay put.'*

*'But grandmother,' pleaded her granddaughter,
'you've no idea what it will be like. They'll be drunk.
They won't even respect old women. Flee with us!'*

*'Enough, enough. Sha!' said granny, 'A pogrom is a
pogrom!'*

This joke I've heard told about all situations of persecution
and hate in many different ways. It's nonetheless true and a
very important joke. A compulsory weapon in the fight
against prejudice.

Modern Times

*The Nazi said to the Jew, 'The Jews are responsible for
all Germany's problems.'*
  'Yes,' said the Jew, 'the Jews and the joggers.'
  'Why the joggers?' said the Nazi puzzled.
  'Why the Jews?' answered the Jew.

But even Anti-Semitism could be laughed at too.

*'I cccccouldn't gggget the the jjjjob,' said the stammer-
ing man. 'Yyyyyou knnnnnow how it is thththese days
if yyyyou're Jjjjjjjewish.'*
  'What job was it?' asked his friend, compassionately.
  *'Rrrrrrrradddddio pppppppppresssentter, of ccccc-
course.'*

Berlin Humour

I refer to the subdued, shabby East Berlin of the Stalinist
years, not to the glitzy Berlin that replaced it after the Wall
came down. Not having to live in it or feel imprisoned by it I
quite enjoyed it. I first went there to see the future but I
soon realised that what I was really seeing was the German
past. It was very polite and rather empty. Like Alice, I had
fallen down a rabbit hole or time warp and lo, I was in the
Kaiser's Germany. Little girls curtseyed to you and people
went out of their way to help if you had lost your way.
Workmen in a pub carefully unfolded plastic squares to sit
on lest their working clothes dirty the chairs. It seemed a
sad but sensible place to retire to, provided you didn't inter-
fere in politics other than signing the appropriate propa-

ganda petition of the moment. After the consumerist orgy in the West, there was something calming about a shop window with one dusty corset and a slogan proclaiming that this was the Future. It was what I imagine Margate to feel like out of season. The jokes were the ways in which people released their exasperation. Naturally they had to be careful whom they told them to.

A man entered an East Berlin butcher's shop. 'I should like some fillet steak,' he said.

'I'm sorry, sir,' said the butcher, 'but it just happens we're out of steak for the moment. But I'm sure some will be coming in next week.' His assistant looked on, amazed.

'Bother!' said the man. 'Well, in that case I'll have some lamb chops instead.'

'The lamb chops have just been sold out,' said the butcher apologetically. 'But I'll put in an order for some immediately.'

The old man then asked in an irritated voice if he could have some pork chops then with the kidney left on. 'Oh my goodness,' said the butcher, 'how unfortunate that I'm out of those too. Come back another time and perhaps I can be of more service.' He politely opened the door and bowed as the grumbling old man left.

'I don't know why you were so polite to him,' said the butcher's assistant. 'We haven't had such things since before the war. What impertinence, what sauce!'

'Ah,' said the butcher with a sigh, 'but what a memory!'

Here's a modern German version of a very old Russian Jewish joke.

After Stalin died, the East German Chancellor went to see Khrushchev in Moscow. 'You've got to pull your socks up,' said Khrushchev. 'You've got to be bright and with it and surround yourself with intelligent young men. I'll test you to see how intelligent you are. Who's my mother's son who's not my brother?'

The Chancellor bit his nails. 'I don't know, Comrade Khrushchev,' he said, distraught.

'Look,' said Khrushchev, 'I'll ask this bright young party member here. Who's my mother's son who's not my brother?' he demanded.

'Simple,' said the bright young aparatchik, 'It can only be yourself, Comrade Khrushchev.'

'That's right,' said Khrushchev. 'Now remember, back in Berlin get rid of the old party hacks and surround yourself with bright young men like this.'

Back in Berlin the Chancellor gloomily summoned his deputy to him. 'Khrushchev told me in Moscow that I must surround myself with bright young men. Well, you're not young but let's see how bright you are. Answer me this question, 'Who's your mother's son who's not your brother?'

The deputy wrung his hands. 'I don't know, Comrade Chancellor,' he cried. 'Who is it?'

'Well,' said the Chancellor, thoughtfully, 'Khrushchev says it's him – but what his reasons are I don't exactly understand.'

✴

After the Soviet cosmonaut Gagarin came back to earth, he was feted all over the USSR, with the climax to all the celebrations in Red Square in Moscow. After the parties were over, he received a note that Khrushchev wanted to see him, but very privately.

'I don't know how to put this, Comrade Gagarin, but I need to ask you a very private question.'

'I think I know what you want to ask, Comrade Khrushchev,' said Gagarin.

'Very well, Comrade Gagarin, when you were up there, did you see Him, does He exist?'

'I did and He does,' said Gagarin.

'Hmmm ...' said Khrushchev. 'I always thought that might be the case but for the sake of our country and our party I must ask you, Comrade, to swear never to tell this to anybody.'

Gagarin swears.

He is then sent to all the great cities of the world where he is again feted by their leaders.

In one of them a great religious leader asks to see him, but privately. 'Mr Gagarin,' he says, 'I don't know quite how to put this but I have a very embarrassing question to ask.' He pauses.

'I think I know what you want to ask,' says Gagarin.

'Well, when you were up there did you see Him, does He exist?'

'No, your holy eminence,' answered Gagarin. 'I didn't and He doesn't.'

'Hmmm ...' said the great religious leader. 'I always thought that might be the case but for the sake of world peace and our co-existence, I must ask you to swear never to tell this to anybody.'

The bewildered Gagarin swears.

Three men are condemned by a revolutionary tribunal in Moscow. Each was asked for his last wish.

'Put my ashes next to Lenin's,' said the first man.

'Put my ashes next to Stalin's,' said the second.

'Put my ashes next to Bertha Rosenberg's,' said the third.

The commandant looks puzzled. 'But Bertha Rosenberg is still alive,' said the commandant.

'So I'll wait,' said the third.

Towards the end of the Communist era, some of the jokes got very black indeed.

As the regime crumbled and the problems of the new era got worse, a group of old comrades, driven to desperation, finally decided to pray to the spirit of Stalin.

'Comrade Stalin,' they intoned, 'come back to us. Without your guidance the Soviets are crumbling. We need you for the sake of the party.'

There was silence.

They tried again, even more fervently. 'Oh Comrade Stalin, listen to our prayer. We need you, the state needs you, the party needs you. Come back to us in our misery!'

Suddenly the old terrible voice of Uncle Joe boomed from above. 'Very well,' it said, 'but this time I warn you – no more Mr Nice Guy!'

When I heard the last, I shivered though it was a warm day.

Rothschilds and Beggars

These were the poles by which we measured our economic progress. Rothschilds we never met – except in dreams and jokes of course – but beggars were the familiar figures of my childhood. The Jewish world was not then a class world in the English sense. Some had a lot, some had nothing. It didn't matter socially because everybody knew that another small turn of the political wheel and we could all become refugees again, begging not just for coins but for our lives. Stencl, one of the greatest Yiddish poets, slept on a park bench nearby. It was his bad luck that his readership went up in the smoke of the gas chambers.

When I had a breakdown during my student years, I thought I might end up as a beggar outside a food or department store. I just couldn't cope with life. Fortunately I found God and a psychoanalyst found me. Though I am 'comfortable' now, I never take it for granted.

The Rothschilds did a lot to help the poor Jewish immigrants pouring in from the pogroms of Eastern Europe. Though in high society, they never disowned their poor relations. So our remarks about them were kind and appreciative, though a world separated us from them.

In the ladies' gallery of the synagogue a woman points out a young boy in the seats below. 'He's a Rothschild!' she said knowingly. 'My God,' said the other, overcome by emotion and awe. 'Oh my! So young and a Rothschild already. Would you believe it!'

A lady, overwhelmed by the splendour of a Rothschild funeral, smacked her lips and said, 'Now that's what I call living!'

A Rothschild sees a man selling pickled herrings from a barrow in Petticoat Lane for a penny a herring. On his next visit to the market he asks the man how much they are. 'For you a special price,' said the man, beaming, 'sixpence a herring.' 'What!' said Lord Rothschild, 'are herrings now so scarce in Petticoat Lane?' 'No,' said the man, 'but visiting Rothschilds are!'

Exactly the same repartee went on with beggars. They had their place in poor Jewish society and were expected to answer back and entertain.

A lady gives a beggar some slices of bread. He chews it critically. 'It's not as nice as the bread you gave me last week,' he complained. 'That was Sabbath egg bread, which costs twice as much,' she exclaimed indignantly. 'Take it from me, lady,' said the beggar judiciously, 'it's worth every extra penny!'

Sometimes poor people and Rothschilds met in dreams and hopes.

'If I were a Rothschild,' boasted an out of work musician, 'I would be richer than a Rothschild.' 'How come?' asked his wife, puzzled. 'Because I'd do a little playing at weddings on the side!'

Usually the beggar came off best in these encounters.

A lady passing a beggar on the street exclaims, 'I've a principle not to give beggars money on the street.' 'Don't worry lady,' said the beggar, 'I'll open a current bank account before we meet next.'

Mr Cohen says to the beggar apologetically, 'Sorry I came out without any change. I'll give you the usual tomorrow.'

'I can't allow it,' says the beggar, shaking his head firmly. 'That's how I became a beggar in the first place – by extending credit.'

The obligation to give charity was so strong in the pious world I was brought up in that beggars were quite insistent on their rights.

This well-off man was mindful of his charitable obligation and gave to a certain beggar regularly. When the beggar turned up for his weekly charity, the man was apologetic. 'I'm sorry,' he said penitently, 'but I've got no change left. I've just come back from seeing my children off to holiday camp. And you know how it is with

children, they wanted comics, chocolate and pop for the
journey in case the buffet car closed and I had to pay for
them.'

The beggar glared back at him, shaking with fury.
'What, with my money!' he shouted.

Nowadays beggars have become more sophisticated, like all
of us, and it is difficult to discern the 'genuine' beggar from
the other sort. I give food now not money. Sometimes it's
rejected but then they've been through such a lot of rejec-
tion, it's only fair for them to want to return it.

Mrs Cohen gives all her loose change to a sad, worn out
beggar. Later on, after her shopping, she sees the same
beggar coming out of a delicatessen with a smile on his
face, smacking his lips and munching a smoked salmon
sandwich. She is scandalised and accosts him. 'I didn't
give you my hard-earned money to buy smoked salmon.
You should be ashamed of yourself.'

'Look, madam,' said the beggar resignedly. 'When I
haven't got the money I can't buy smoked salmon and
when I have got the money I mustn't buy smoked
salmon.' His voice rises in anger. 'So when do I ever get
the chance to eat smoked salmon, tell me that?'

The beggar won that round but I think the donor won this.

The beggar approaches a lady and says to her piteously,
'Madam, I haven't had a bite to eat for three days.' The
lady looks at him with commiseration. 'Poor man, force
yourself!' she says to him compassionately, 'you must
force yourself!'

10

Places

At the Party

If you're just going out to dinner, there's a ring at the door and three people are outside claiming you've invited them to eat with you that night, remember that God also created the fish and chip shop. No white lies, just confess! It's easier for everybody and better for your soul.

You can also phone the people you were supposed to be dining with to warn them that they will now have to divide five salmon steaks into eight portions. Be brave, be honest! Tell them that God, you and the guests will all repay them in kind or with continuous prayers for their souls. Some nuns I knew didn't turn a hair and I'm still benefiting from their example twelve years on.

> 'Why, what lovely little canapés!' exclaimed the guest, selecting yet another. 'Did you make them yourself? I've already eaten five!'
>
> 'Six,' said her hostess judiciously, 'but who's counting?' she added gaily.

> At the party a guest couldn't help staring at two beautiful sisters.
>
> Before he left he went to his hostess and asked her to convey his compliments to them.

'*I've never before seen two women so alike and so lovely.*'

To his surprise his hostess curtly refused. '*They're no sisters.*' she said briefly. '*They just go to the same plastic surgeon, that's all!*'

At the Concert Hall

The new concerto is about to be played – Goldberg's 1st. The orchestra have tuned their instruments, the soloist has bowed to the audience but just as the conductor is raising his baton the soloist suddenly collapses. The conductor rushes over to him and calls out urgently, 'Is there a doctor in the house?'

A lady in the gallery calls out too. 'Give him an enema, give him an enema!' she cries tearfully. The conductor ignores her.

A doctor in the audience rushes forward, examines the soloist, and whispers earnestly to the conductor.

'*I'm afraid it's very serious,*' *announces the conductor sadly to the audience. But before he could continue, the imploring voice again moans from the gallery, 'Give him an enema, give him an enema!'*

'*Be quiet up there!*' *shouts back the distracted conductor.*

The doctor again comes to speak to him and the conductor sorrowfully announces that the soloist is dead. 'Give him an enema, Oh give him an enema!' the woman cries from the gallery.

Goaded beyond endurance the conductor shouts

back, '*Keep quiet! What good would an enema do?*'
'*It wouldn't do any harm,*' says the lady reasonably.

The little boy urges his grandpa to take him to the concert.
'*They put the violinist inside a gun,*' he says, '*and shoot the
gun just as it's time for his entry.*' The grandpa pooh-
poohs the story but is curious and goes along nevertheless.

It happened just as the boy said. Before the violin concerto started the soloist was stuffed inside a cannon and
was shot out as his solo part began, continuing to play
the violin as he curved through the air.

'*Wasn't that wonderful, grandpa?*' said the little boy
with tears in his eyes.

'*Interesting, interesting,*' admitted his grandpa grudgingly. '*Now Menuhin plays it better!*'

Just as the concert is about to begin, a woman shouts
out, '*Is there a doctor in the house?*' and collapses. A
young doctor rushes forward and bends over her.

She looks up at him soulfully. '*Doctor,*' she whispers
enticingly, '*have I got a lovely girl for you!*'

At the Pub

The customer enters the pub accompanied by his pet
ostrich. '*A pint of bitter for me and a gin for my ostrich,*'
he orders. A few minutes later he repeats this order and

later on yet again. The customer seems able to hold his liquor but not so the poor ostrich, which collapses onto the floor in a heap of feathers.

The publican is worried. 'You can't leave that'un lyin' here yer know,' he said in a worried voice.

'It's not a lion,' said the man belligerently. 'It's my pet ostrich!'

A man enters a pub with his parrot and orders himself a double. 'We don't serve apes in this house,' says the publican.

'It's not an ape, it's a parrot,' said the customer self-righteously.

'I was talking to the parrot,' said the publican.

These jokes were told to me in pubs. In a 'bruin café' in Amsterdam I asked for a Dutch joke but nobody could think of one. They could only remember jokes about Germans and Belgians. Anyway, here is one they told me about Germans.

Late in life Herr and Frau Schmidt have a child called Siegfried. He is a lovely child, nice looking and trouble free. But as he grows his parents realise with horror that he never speaks or cannot speak. He is examined by ear specialists, throat specialists and child psychiatrists but all are bewildered. They cannot find anything wrong. He just doesn't speak.

When Siegfried is five years old and the family are having supper, he lays down his soup spoon and says clearly and distinctly, 'Die Suppe ist kalt' (the soup is cold). His parents look at him amazed and his mother bursts into tears.

'Why, you can speak!' they shout and sob. 'Why haven't you ever spoken before?'

'Bis jezt,' replies Siegfried, detachedly, 'war alles in ordnung' (until now, everything was fine).

Although the Dutch didn't seem to have their own jokes, one Dutchman I met said they didn't need them because they still enjoyed the Jewish jokes from before the war and occupation. Many of them concerned a character called Mose who is still famous in Amsterdam.

Mose goes to Rome and as soon as he gets there an invitation arrives from the Vatican. 'Why didn't you tell us you were coming, Mose?' writes His Holiness, 'You must come for tea straight away.'

As Mose is taking tea with the Pope an enormous cheering takes place outside. 'Let's go out on the balcony, Mose,' His Holiness says to him. They appear together and the crowd below goes frantic. A bewildered Japanese tourist, conscientiously taking photos, turns to a Dutchman nearby and asks who's up there on the balcony.

'Well,' said the Dutchman, 'the man on the right is our famous Mose from Amsterdam.' He shook his head, 'But who the other one is I'm not quite sure.'

The following anecdote was also told to me in a café – in Geneva by a genial Swiss. I have a liking for Swiss people and it was nice to know that they could even take the mickey out of themselves.

When God created the world, he asked all the peoples what they would like.

'I would like mountains,' said the Swiss man and suddenly Alps and mountains were everywhere,

'And what else would you like?' said God.

'I would like meadows with cows,' said the Swiss man. And suddenly the slopes of the Alps were clothed in meadows full of cows.

The Swiss man, overcome with happiness, rushed to them and started to milk one of the cows. He was just about to drink a beaker full of milk, when a thought struck him. Turning to God, he said shyly, 'Would you like one?'

'Yes, please,' said God gratefully, deeply moved by the gift, 'Thank you so much.'

'One franc please,' said the Swiss man.

America

At the turn of the century a tidal wave of the poor, persecuted and dispossessed fled Europe, making for Ellis Island and, if they were lucky, the Golden Country that lay beyond. Some didn't make it and only got half way like my grandparents, which is why I was born in London, England not London, USA – a limey not a yankee. (I don't regret it though, because I love this country of my birth.) This little snatch of conversation recalls the longings of those times.

'Mummy, mummy, must I go to America?' said the child.

'Don't waste your strength arguing my darling, save it and just keep on swimming,' replied its mother.

Of course the New World could seem very strange compared to the pieties of the old one and it was often the little things which seemed so important.

A young rabbinical student emigrates across the Atlantic to avoid conscription in the Tsarist armies. Over there he becomes a businessman and strikes it rich. So rich that he eventually brings his mother over too. She is dazzled by his lifestyle and his riches. Eventually she plucks up courage to ask him a question that's needling her. 'Son,' she says hesitantly, 'you don't seem to pray three times a day any more?'

'Ma, life over here is so fast there's no time between business meetings. That's the way it is if you want to get on.'

'Son,' she said hopefully, 'but you still eat kosher don't you?'

'Ma, in this great country, you have to mix, you can't separate yourself from your associates. That's the way it is.'

His mother broods over his answers. 'Just one more question, my son,' she cried piteously, 'Are you still circumcised?'

Places

A pious young man, with the blessing of his rabbi, decided to leave the old country and try to make his way in America. Before he left he asked his old rabbi to give him some words of wisdom to carry over the Atlantic in his heart.

'Always remember,' said the rabbi, 'that life is a precious flower of purest gold.'

In America the young man made his fortune and whenever he lost confidence he just repeated to himself the words of his holy rabbi on parting, that this life was like a precious flower with petals of the purest gold.

Eventually, he did so well that he brought his old rabbi across the Atlantic to join him. When they were alone together, the young man said, 'Rabbi, through all these years I've been away I've just wanted to ask you one question. I've often thought of your words of encouragement before I left the old country and they helped me through many dark days here. May I ask you one more question?' 'Ask it, my dear pupil!' said the rabbi warmly. 'Oh, my master,' said the young man, 'can you tell me what you meant when you said that this life is like a precious flower with petals of the purest gold?'

The rabbi became silent and then querulous and sulky. 'OK,' he said wearily, 'so it isn't like a precious flower with petals of the purest gold – so what!'

11

Identifiably Jewish

You Don't Look Jewish!

Most persecuted people take on the distortions and prejudices of their persecutors. Even Jews today sometimes think
of themselves as a 'race', which they are not. It is doubtful if
even the tiniest fraction of a per cent of Abraham's blood
flows in theirs and North European Jews have more Slav,
Germanic and Khazar than Semitic characteristics.

*A Jewish tourist from Golders Green took a package holi-
day to China. To his surprise, the guide led him to a synagogue, and he watched the congregation, astonished.*

'Are you real Jews?' he asked the beadle.

*'We're very strict kosher-keeping Jews,' answered the
beadle huffily. 'But please, it's been bothering me, are
you Jewish too?'*

'Of course,' said the tourist. 'Why do you ask?'

*'Because you just don't look Jewish,' said the beadle,
scrutinising him, puzzled, and shaking his head.*

*Two men, both taking their dogs out for a walk, meet
each other in the park. One has a fierce big Alsatian
type dog and the other a low-slung dachshund type.*

*'You'd better keep your little pet away from mine,'
says the first grandly. 'Mine might do it a mischief.'*

'Oh, mine can take care of itself,' says the other.

At that moment the big dog growled and the little dog snapped and the owner of the big dog was left with just a stump of dog lead in his hand. 'My God,' he said, shaking all over, 'what sort of dog is that?'

'Well,' said the other nonchalantly, 'it's not really a dog. It's an alligator but we gave him an expensive nose job!'

Incidentally, the stories you hear about Jewish looks are mostly fictitious. My nose is snub, like my father's. My mother's was classic, like her father's. It's a painful subject for Jews, which is why they turn it into jokes.

An old Jewish woman in the underground sees a black chap reading a Yiddish newspaper. She is fascinated. 'Excuse me, Mr Black,' she says politely, 'but can you be Jewish?' The black chap spreads out his hands and shrugs his shoulders. 'Lady,' he replies in Yiddish, 'Dos faeltst mir noch!' (Which means – 'Madam, that's all I need!')

Here's a return match.

A West African lady tries on a fur coat in an expensive West End store. 'Why, what a wonderful fit!' says the attendant, 'Madam is beautiful in it.' The African lady gazes at the coat in the mirror. 'Don't you think it makes me look a little too Jewish?' she says critically.

Such jokes are of course not politically correct, though really they are quite self-critical. But in for a penny in for a pound, so let's go the whole hog so to speak – you should pardon the expression – and say what is religiously incorrect as well. Rabbi Hugo Gryn (may his memory be for blessing!) whispered this to me during an extraordinarily tedious meeting about the constitution of a committee.

> *A new immigrant in America stops another man in the street, whom he thinks looks Jewish, and asks, 'Excuse me, is this state pronounced Wisconsin or Visconcin?'*
>
> *'Visconsin, of course,' said the other, everyone knows that!'*
>
> *'Thank you, sir,' said the man.*
>
> *'It's nuttink,' said the other, 'you're velcome!'*

Bertholt Brecht, the German writer and refugee from the Nazis, said that his generation had to change their country more often than their shoes. And he was right. The evidence is left on Jewish speech and it takes a generation or two to get it right. For example, I still say 'thinkink' not 'thinking', a left-over from my early Yiddish and Cockney. The 'H' caused great trouble. In Russian it was replaced by a 'G' and in Cockney it was sometimes silent and sometimes sounded. The missing or overstated 'H' became a standard target of jokes – hobviously!

> *As Mrs Levy was buying food for the festival in the market, she shouted across to Mrs Cohen, 'Oh boy, 'ave I got a haddock 'ere!' And Mrs Cohen replied, 'Hev a hesprin, Mrs Levy, 'ere's a hesprin. Hit's a hentidote!'*

Identifiably Jewish

The pious old man and his wife from Jewish East London take the first holiday in their lives, she worn out by work, he worn out by study. Timorously they join their cruise boat in Florida, she dressed in black shawls and the wig demanded by piety, he with long ear locks and garbed in a black gabardine coat with a black brimmed hat. Their fellow cruisers, clad, if you can call it that, in bikinis and thongs, see them and burst into helpless laughter.

She is frightened and clutches her husband. 'What are they jeering at us for? What have we done?' she asks, frightened.

He reassures her. 'Nothing, nothing, darling, my beautiful one. Perhaps down here, they've never set eyes on real Brits like us before.'

Why do you think non-Jewish wives convert? With a Jewish wife you get false orgasms and real diamonds. With a non-Jewish wife it's vice versa!

Subversive Religion

Don't trust religion, even your own, or especially your own if it can't take a joke. That's a sign of insecurity. Perhaps you don't believe as much as you would like to. If so it's better to have it out and face it. Your religion has to grow up just like you.

A Jewish boy is marrying a very traditional girl. Because he is not that observant himself, he goes to her rabbi to find out what is permissible in very traditional circles. 'Can we dance together at the reception after the ceremony?' he asks. 'No,' said the rabbi solemnly, 'dancing is lascivious!'

'Can we make love in our room afterwards?' said the worried groom. 'Sure,' said the rabbi, 'the more you make love the better. God wants it! Be fruitful and multiply!'

'Can we make love on the floor before we go to bed?' asks the groom daringly. 'Why not,' said the rabbi. 'Do it as often as possible. That's what marriage is about.'

'Can we do it standing up then – in the lift for example?' asked the daring groom. 'Never!' declaimed the rabbi severely, putting him down firmly. 'That might lead to dancing!'

The Unauthorised Version of Some Jewish Religious Festivals

Religious festivals pack a powerful punch and sometimes a dangerous one. They cannot help it, containing as they do exclusive elements, myths, tendentious history and the dreams of previous generations often linked to modern nationalism and even to political attitudes and programmes. This does not negate their magic, their love and the self-sacrifice they teach. The unauthorised jokes cleanse them with humour and common sense.

The little boy returned from religious classes, where he had been taught the story of Passover. 'And what did the teacher tell you?' asked his beaming parents. 'Well,' said the little boy, 'when the Children of Israel came to the Red Sea, little green Moonmen landed in space ships and with the help of yellow submarines they got all the Children of Israel across.'

'Is that what the teacher really taught you?' asked his amazed and upset parents.

'Not exactly,' said their son reluctantly, 'but if I tell you how they got across as he told it, then you wouldn't believe a word of it!'

At the Jewish New Year, sweet apple is eaten as a sign that the coming year should be sweet for you.

Members of a synagogue, passing by a very non-kosher restaurant at New Year time, look through its windows in curiosity. They are stupefied when they see their rabbi making merry at the top table.

They rush in and confront him. 'How can you be in such a place at such a time?' they ask, scandalised.

'Oh, I'm not here for the food,' he stammers. 'I'm here for the culture and the sophistication. Look at the beautiful silver and furniture. I'm here for the aesthetic experience.'

Suddenly the lights are turned low, there is the skirl of bagpipes and to the horror of the members of his congregation, a flaming boar's head is brought in on a salver.

'Oh, look,' said the rabbi weakly, 'with what art and style they present the New Year apple!'

On the fast of the Day of Atonement all work and games are forbidden – only prayers and religious study are allowed. But it is a beautiful September day and Mr Cohen, who wakes up early, looks at the golf course through his window and cannot resist playing a round on his own. He could do it before anyone got up so no one would ever know.

But of course the angels on high knew and protested to God about it – Mr Cohen being after all the President of the local congregation. 'Aren't you going to stop him?' they said to God. 'Not at all,' he answered, 'Don't be so impatient, wait!'

To the angels' amazement Mr Cohen went round the course from triumph to triumph. Never had he completed the course in so few strokes. It was a wonder. Mr Cohen was ecstatic.

This enraged the angels even more and again they protested to God, who let them have their say and simply smiled.

'And who do you think he'll ever dare tell his triumph to?' God said quietly and laughed.

I used to have a problem with the Day of Atonement. I started off the service by addressing God in front of the Ark and confessing to Him that I was just a fleeting shadow, a passing cloud, little more than nothing.

But it wasn't so easy believing it because the synagogue was full with standing room only, the silver in the Ark was shining, the usual choir was augmented and I was wearing my newly laundered white robes. I mentioned my spiritual problem to one of my wardens who told me this story. Each year I tell it to myself before the great fast commences and it helps me become humble. This was his story:

> *The Day of Atonement service was about to begin when the congregation was startled as the rabbi halted the service, descended from his pulpit, went to the Holy Ark and prostrated himself before it. 'Lord,' he said, 'I am a passing cloud, a fleeting shadow, just dust and ashes.' The congregation is deeply moved as he rises up slowly and ascends his pulpit in silence.*
>
> *Once again the service is about to begin when the cantor this time raises his hand for silence and the congregation is moved once more as he descends from his pulpit, opens the Holy Ark, prostrates himself like the rabbi and says sorrowfully, 'Lord, I too am but dust and ashes.' They watch him raise himself up slowly and return to his pulpit.*
>
> *Yet once again the service is about to start when a voice is heard from the back of the synagogue, from the beadle, the lowest of the low in the synagogue hierarchy. He too opens the Ark, bows before it and says hurriedly, 'Lord, I'm also dust and ashes.' He promptly closes the Ark and quickly scuttles back to his place by the door.*
>
> *The rabbi then turns to the cantor and in a superior voice says disdainfully, 'Just look who dares think he is also dust and ashes!'*

Jewish Humour

The Jewish world is a small world and every so often fresh waves of humour ripple through it. Synagogue wardens whisper it to rabbis, who whisper it to other rabbis during the interminable committee meetings, which are part of ecclesiastical and communal life. That's certainly where I acquire many of my favourite jokes. But they in turn are variations on themes that go back to unknown tellers who heard them from the lips of other unknown tellers. The humour need not be in the words but in the person who tells them and how she or he tells them.

There were the JAP jokes. Now JAPs are not members of a nationality but of a class, an upper moneyed class. They are the spoilt daughters of wealthy transatlantic daddies – in America originally but now everywhere. Now you've got the clue you should be able to decipher the word yourself – Jewish American Princesses. Easy, when you know how!

What does a JAP make for dinner parties? Reservations of course!

How does a JAP indicate a climax of passion? She lets go her eyeliner!

There are many, many more but you can make your own CAPs – spoilt Christian daughters maybe.

I think the most instructive wave of jokes are those concerning light bulbs. Who originated them remains for me a mystery, but they have become handy pegs for theology, ingenuity and self-criticism.

How many rabbis does it take to change a light bulb? A working party full, to organise a conference of electri-

144

cians, commentators on Genesis Chapter 1, verse 3, DIY enthusiasts, religious legal experts, theologians and mystics following their inner light.

How many olde tyme rabbis does it take to change a light bulb? Change! How can you say such a blasphemous word? Wash your mouth out!

Or, visiting the other end of the Jewish spectrum:

How many reform rabbis does it take to change a light bulb? Who needs a rabbi? Let each congregant decide for herself!

There are of course many variations and refinements.

How many mystics does it take to change a light bulb? Please, what's a light bulb? It doesn't say in the Cabbalah? We always rely on our inner light.

How many Chelmites does it take to change a light bulb? (Chelm was traditionally a village of dim pious Jews.) Three! One to fit the bulb in and two to turn the chair he's standing on!

Nobody, and no section of the community, gets spared. Rabbis dream them up at those interminable meetings I've mentioned.

How many Zionists does it take to change a light bulb? At least three! One to act as fundraiser to pay for someone to emigrate to Israel while the third denounces it as a political plot!

My own favourite?

How many Jewish mothers does it take to change a light bulb? None! Don't bother about me – I'll just sit in the dark!

And there are some for the sophisticated, secular Jews too.

How many Jewish psychoanalysts does it take to change a light bulb? Only one – provided of course the light bulb really wants to change!

How many hippies does it take to change a light bulb? A squatful! One to change the bulb and the rest of the squat to share the experience.

Now make up your own with ecumenical clerical colleagues.

How many hermits does it take to change a light bulb? How many cardinals? How many evangelists? How many Mothers Superior?...Off you go!

12
Clergy, People and Other Animals

None So Queer as Folk

'There's so much bad in the best of us
And so much good in the worst of us
That it ill behoves any of us
To talk about the rest of us!'
(Lines I learnt as a child in the West Country.)

Which of course doesn't stop us talking about them one bit! And such talk is good because it reminds us that neither we nor they are complete goodies or baddies but all of us in-between people living in an in-between world. The baddies are often just those who happen to get in our way. Unless you're dealing with the Hitlers of this world – fortunately they're few – the mixture of good and bad makes people human and very funny. So enjoy them if you can.

'Your reverence,' said the man to the priest, 'I felt I had to tell you about poor Mrs Kelly on the floor above me. Her clothes are worn out, she's got hardly anything to eat – she can't even pay her rent.'

'How good of you to come to me,' says the priest. 'I'll organise a collection for her. Are you a relation of hers?'

147

'No,' said the man. 'Then you must be her good friend.'
'No,' admitted the man 'I hardly know her.'

'Then how wonderful,' said the minister, 'that you're so concerned you've taken this trouble. How do you know about her situation?'

'I'm her landlord,' said the man simply.

'If I found a thousand pounds lying in the gutter,' said the rabbi grandly, 'I would hand it in to the police without another thought, provided the person who lost it was a poor man of course.'

A lady talking about her holiday. 'And the hotel food was diabolical, sheer poison – and, my dear, such small portions too!'

Pious and Profane Laughter – How Funny Religion Can Be!

I think the source of the laughter stems from the fact that we grow up and become adult but a lot of our religion doesn't. It seems locked Peter Pan-like in its Sunday school state. It is not God we're laughing at (though He might find it a delightful change after all the dirges and unoriginal sins He has to listen to) but our undeveloped ideas about Him and His work in our world. The more secure you are in your religion, the less such jokes will trouble you. Actually they're more than jokes. Many of them are worth hours of knee work.

> *A Jewish chap is shipwrecked and only discovered years later when a passing cruise ship sees his white distress flag from the distance. When he meets the sailors he can hardly contain himself and, beside himself with relief and joy, he gives them a tour of his little island. One of them notices a beautifully built hut on a hill. 'Is that the home you built to live in?' he asks respectfully. 'No,' says the man reverently, 'that's the synagogue I built to pray in.'*
>
> *The sailors are impressed. One of them then notices another hill, also with a beautifully built hut on it. 'Is that the home you built to live in then?' he asks.*
>
> *'Oh no,' says the man disdainfully, 'that's the synagogue I wouldn't be seen dead in!'*

In a materialist age 'religious objects' often mean more than religious actions. This is what has happened in Jerusalem. People prefer their religion material and solid to spiritual and see-through. So there are too many religious objects and not enough religious deeds. Therefore, this story about the Wailing Wall – all that remains of Herod's Second Temple.

> *A Japanese tourist gazes with admiration at the pious praying before the stones of the Wailing Wall. He goes up to one and politely enquires if he often comes to pray at these holy stones.*

'Sure,' says the man, 'I pray here two or three times a week like my father and grandfather before me.'

'And what do you pray for?' asks the tourist humbly.

'Peace for Israel, peace for all mankind,' answers the man simply.

'Thank you so much,' said the tourist. But, just as he was about to go, he turned and said, 'May I ask you one more question?'

'Sure,' said the man, 'go ahead and ask!'

'Do your prayers before these holy stones ever get answered?'

'Nah,' replied the exasperated worshipper, 'between ourselves it's like talking to a brick wall!'

In this synagogue some sat for the 'Hear, O Israel' prayer. And others stood up for it. Tempers got frayed and the worshippers began to throw prayer books at each other. Both sides then agreed to abide by the original tradition of the congregation. But who knew it? Someone then remembered one of the congregation's founder members now in an old age home and the leaders of both parties rushed over to see him.

The sit-downer explained his custom. The old man said hesitantly, 'No, the tradition wasn't exactly like that.'

The stand-upper then explained his custom. 'No,' said the old man, 'it wasn't like that either.'

'Please remember,' both pleaded, 'we can't go on. Every service turns into a rough house and our worshippers throw books at each other.'

The old man's face suddenly lit up. 'I remember, I remember,' he mumbled excitedly. 'That's exactly what it was like,' he said, beaming at them happily. 'That was our tradition!'

A long line of people are queuing outside the pearly gates, waiting to be processed. A self-important old man with a sheaf of papers and a mobile pushes his way to the front and is immediately let in.

The queue becomes restive. 'What's so special about him?' one calls out to a passing angel.

'Sh...' said the horrified angel, 'that's the Almighty Himself. But sometimes,' whispers the angel, 'between you and me He gets a bit megalo and thinks He's a spin doctor.'

Animals

From ancient times people have told stories about animals to make fun of themselves and their fellow human beings. In such stories the animal usually gets the last laugh.

A rabbit enters a chemist's shop. 'Have you any carrots?' he asks politely. 'This is a chemist's not a greengrocer's,' says the man.

The next day the rabbit pops in again. 'Have you any carrots?' he asks. 'I told you this is a chemist's not a greengrocer's,' says the man angrily. 'If you come in and ask me again, I'll nail your ears to the counter.'

The following day the rabbit sidles in once more. 'Have you any nails?' he asks nervously. The man shakes his head. 'Then have you any carrots?' asks the rabbit perkily.

The greatest joke was a discussion I overheard some time after telling this story on the radio. One person said, 'I couldn't understand the religious point of that joke the rabbi told about the rabbit.' 'Oh,' said the other, 'I thought it was obvious that he was referring to the crucifixion' !!!!!!

The rabbi is late for the evening service and no one is sure what to do. 'Don't worry,' said an old man. 'My dog will take the service.' 'Your dog!' they said. 'Sure,' said the old man and he called to his dog beside him.

The dog promptly padded down the aisle, put his paws on the reading desk, barked for silence and then growled his way through the liturgy. When it was finished, the dog inclined his muzzle respectfully, barked 'Amen,' and made his way back to his master.

The congregation was so impressed they gathered round the old man to congratulate him. 'Why,' said one, 'that dog should become a rabbi.' 'You tell him,' said the man sorrowfully. 'He wants to get his own website.'

The following is a traditional, simple but therapeutic joke always worth bearing in mind.

'I can't take it any more, rabbi,' says the poor man. 'My wife complains, and the children shriek and I can never get any rest. What shall I do?'

'Buy some hens!' says the rabbi.

The man does as he is bidden but again calls on the rabbi. 'It's even worse now,' he says. 'When my wife complains not only do the children shriek but the hens cluck. I'm at my wits' end.'

'Buy a dog!' says the sage.

The man looks astonished but does what his rabbi says and returns a few days later, worn out. 'Have mercy, rabbi,' he pleads. 'Now not only do the hens cluck but the dog barks and I want to die.'

'Buy a goat,' orders the merciless sage.

A few days later the man returns, broken and sobbing. 'My wife complains, the children shriek, the dog barks and now the goat bleats and I'm going out of my mind. Have pity, rabbi! Have pity!' and he weeps.

'Very well,' says the rabbi, 'sell the chickens, the dog and the goat.'

Some days later the man returns again. 'Life's so wonderful now,' he says. 'Without all that clucking, barking and bleating, I think I'm in paradise it's so peaceful. Thank you, rabbi, thank you.'

And he walked out, upright and happy.

As the elderly man walks along the road, he hears someone call out to him. 'Good evening, sir!' He looks around but doesn't see anybody and again the voice calls out, 'Good evening, sir!'

He looks more carefully and sees a frog by the roadside. 'Were you calling?' he asks, astonished. 'I didn't know frogs could talk.'

'I'm not a frog really,' says the frog. *'I'm a lovely young woman whom a wicked witch has turned into a frog.'*

'Can't someone break her spell?' says the agitated old man.

'You could,' replied the frog, *'if you gave me a loving kiss tonight. Then tomorrow morning I would be a lovely young woman again.'*

The old man takes the frog back home, puts it on his bedside table, undresses, says, 'Goodnight frog!' and is just about to put out the light, when the frog cries out, 'Aren't you going to give me a loving kiss?'

'I've been thinking,' says the old man apologetically, *'at my age, you know, I'd far prefer a talking frog.'*

And here is another version with a young prince and a vicar.

'Good evening, your reverence,' says the frog.

The vicar can hardly believe his ears. 'I didn't know frogs could talk,' he says.

'I'm not a frog really,' says the frog. *'I'm a handsome young prince whom a wicked witch has turned into a frog until I sleep one night beside a holy man.'*

'I'll be as holy as I can,' says the vicar humbly and at home he places the frog on the table beside him as he goes to sleep.

Sure enough, when he wakes up the next morning the frog has gone and a handsome young prince lies in its place.

'AND THERE, M'LUD,' boomed the Counsel for the defence, *'THE DEFENCE RESTS ITS CASE!'*

Clergy

It is not easy to criticise directly unless you wrap your criticism in a joke. But all people who have power need criticism and the more power they have the more criticism they should hear. But be kind about it. Clerics don't have an easy job and if you wrap your criticism in a joke it takes away the aggression and makes it easier to accept.

In the middle of the sermon, a man gets up and starts to leave. The preacher is upset and angry. 'Where are you going, my man?' he says, pointing at him.

'I'm going to get a haircut,' replies the man.

'Shouldn't you have thought of that before my sermon started,' said the preacher, reproachfully.

'When your sermon started, your reverence,' says the man, 'I didn't need a haircut!'

The old man snored right the way through the sermon. The young minister couldn't contain his annoyance and shook him. 'You didn't hear one word of the sermon that I spent hours preparing,' he said. 'Ah,' said the old man ingratiatingly, 'that just shows how much I trust you!'

The old boy slept through the entire service. 'Wake him up!' the rabbi ordered the warden. 'You put him to sleep, so you wake him up yourself!' the warden retorted.

The clergy are treated both very well and very badly. They are given low salaries but high status. Congregants will, of course, criticise them remorselessly to each other but boast about their own minister to all other congregations. I think the faithful have the same attitude to them as communities have to their football teams. The ambiguity is inevitable because they are looked upon as father figures and therefore attract the same conflicts that arise between adolescent children and their parents. God is also a parent figure and gets the same treatment. When I started out I was given this piece of professional advice: any Jewish congregation which does not try to get rid of its rabbi is not really Jewish and any rabbi who lets them get away with it is no rabbi. An example of the curious uses to which the clergy are put is as follows.

A rabbi was called to a dying lady in hospital. 'Is there anything I can do for you?' he asked. 'Yes,' she said, 'lots.' 'Take a piece of paper,' she ordered, 'and note these down.' She then proceeded to give him a list of what should not be distributed among her nearest but obviously not her dearest after her demise. He had been expecting her to ask him for the consolations of religion but either she didn't believe in them or didn't want his. He wrote down the list but it soured him. 'Don't you think,' he said smoothly, 'you need the services of a solicitor not a rabbi?' 'Sure,' she said triumphantly, 'but use your common sense. What solicitor would come out at three in the morning.'

Game, set and match to her!

I always refused to get involved in the choosing of my replacement. I just listened and got a liberal education.

'We need a rabbi badly,' said a synagogue warden to his friend from another congregation.

'Take ours!' said his friend urgently. 'Make him an offer he can't refuse. Believe me he's like Shakespeare and Moses in one. He's like an angel. I swear it.'

The warden thanks him for his generosity and unselfishness and immediately reports back to his congregation who make an offer quickly before anyone else discovers this treasure.

The rabbi turns out to be a complete disaster and his sermons are a turn-off, so the warden reproaches his friend bitterly for telling him such a pack of lies. 'How could you say all those things about Shakespeare, Moses, an angel even!'

'I told you the exact truth,' said his friend, now his former friend. 'Shakespeare didn't know Hebrew – neither does he. Moses stammered – so does he. And between ourselves, like an angel he's hardly human!'

The senior warden visits the rabbi in hospital. 'I called to tell you,' he said carefully, 'that our executive at a special meeting passed a resolution wishing you a speedy recovery. Passed twelve for, seven against and nine undecided,' he added hurriedly.

But despite all these professional hazards I have never regretted becoming a minister. I discussed it with a critical rabbi friend and we both agreed it was the best thing we ever could have done. You deal at least, however badly, with big matters and not just the trivia of a rat race society. I feel like this chap who also had a vocation.

At the pub bar a bloke is drinking and then another comes to drink beside him and they start chatting. The second one notices the first one's hands and arms. They are covered with suppurating sores. He can't help asking the first chap how he got them. 'Oh, I work in a circus,' said the first gloomily, 'and it's my job to clean out the animals' throats and bottoms, both ends. Very nervy they are too!'

'But my good man, you can't carry on like that. Why don't you apply for a nice clean job in the Post Office or in a launderette.'

'What,' says the first, highly insulted, 'me! Leave show business – never!'

That's how I feel too!

The clergy are incidentally more in touch with ordinary people and their needs than most of their critics give them credit for. That is why very secular people turn to them in an emergency.

A strange whine was heard through the aeroplane along with a shuddering of the engine. The passengers started to get restive.

'Stop the passengers getting alarmed! Keep them quiet!' the steward hissed to a cleric.

He nodded and without more ado went up and down the aisle taking a collection!

13

Some More Serious Stories

These stories cross the religious frontiers. Forms of them can be found among Jews, Christians and Moslems and I have no doubt they are known in the Far East as well. They probably come from there. I do not know who first told them. The memory is lost.

A rabbi asks God to see heaven and hell. He finds himself in front of a great door, which swings open. He sees a banqueting hall. In the centre of the table is a great pot of delicious smelling stew and around the table are seated the diners. But their spoons are so big that after they fill them they cannot get them to their mouths. So they are screaming with hunger and cursing while God's plenty is before them.

The rabbi is overcome by their cries and begs God to take him away from this hell and give him a sight of heaven.

To his terror he finds himself in front of the same door. It swings open and he is horrified to see the same pot of stew on the same table, the same diners and the same long spoons. But this time they are rejoicing and praising God because they are using those long spoons to feed each other!

That is the only difference between heaven and hell. All the wickedness of the 20th century can be replayed so easily in the 21st if we do not heed its message.

An ascetic and his disciple find their way blocked by a swollen river. A tearful girl is walking up and down the bank not knowing how to cross. The ascetic bends down and gestures for her to mount his shoulders. In that way all three of them cross the river – the girl's legs wound tightly round the ascetic's shoulders, her flesh hard against his.

When they reach the other bank, the ascetic bends down, and the young girl leaps off and thanks him. He never says a word.

The ascetic and his disciple continue their way through the desert. Many times the disciple almost breaks into speech. His master looks at him and the disciple does not continue.

But, later on that evening at their frugal meal, the young man bursts forth. 'How could you carry that young girl on your shoulders,' he demands, 'your neck between her legs, her young flesh pressing into yours?' His master gazed at him. 'So,' he said surprised, 'you are still carrying her!'

I was told about a Japanese saying, which said that the most difficult thing in life is to let go. And this is very true. People can forget their past happiness but rarely their past unhappiness or their suffering.

This is an old Jewish story that states a great truth about our failings and how we can use them. It isn't a joke but it's comforting and reader friendly.

There was once a king who had a beautiful diamond and he was very proud of it because it was unique. But one day the diamond got deeply scratched and nobody could remove the scratch or repair the flaw and the king was very sad.

Then a jeweller came along who said he could make the diamond even better than it was before. The king believed him and entrusted him with his scratched and flawed stone.

And when the workman had finished, the king saw that he had engraved around the flaw a lovely rosebud and the ugly scratch had become the stem.

And here's a workaday story, which is also profound.

Sidney sees Harold tottering round on shoes several sizes too small for him. He's in agony.

'Harold, you've got to buy a bigger pair,' he tells him. 'I can't stand the sight of it. Here's some money!'

'Sidney, I specially bought them like that. You know how bad life's been for me ever since the wife died. Well, when I get home at night and take off these terrible shoes, life suddenly seems so good for me, that I bless God for it.'

Well that's one way of coping with life. It's simple but it works. I think it's the basis of a lot of religious observance.

A Warning

Jokes don't just depend on the words but on the overall situation and the feelings of those who tell them and those who listen to them. They change their message immediately if they are told not *to* people but *at* them or if they publicly show up someone's shortcomings. Because they are told as 'fun' it is very difficult for that someone to contradict or deny them. All of us bear the scars of jokes told against us.

Dean Inge of St Paul's, for example, was a good and kindly man and I admire him but sometimes his wit could overcome his charity which was considerable. He made this remark which was hurtful to self-taught people (like me for example) trying to rise up in life.

'Whom are you?' he said, for he had been to evening classes.

Ouch!

I have included a lot of humorous spiritual material in this book, that is, religious jokes. I have included them not to be flamboyant but because humour can help us laugh away the false gods we all worship at some time or another – nationalist religion, materialist religion, selfish religion, nit-picking religion. When these are gone there is room for true, honest, self-critical, kind religion to grow in us.

I have also included many jokes and anecdotes that can help us laugh away the false images we have of ourselves, mocking the dishonesty and falsity we all resort to in the course of our lives. Once again, not to hurt – they are after all mostly the products of our own insecurity! When they are laughed away we shall feel freer to be ourselves, our super-natural as well as our natural selves. They release us from the past. No more excuses! No more special pleading!

Criticism in the form of jokes is not 'preachy'. The reader and listener can decide themselves whether and how far it is relevant to their situation. It is a good way to enjoy the truth about those parts of oneself respectable sermons don't reach. So enjoy, enjoy!

L'Envoi

I start to tell another story:

'Hymie and Sollie were going along to a bar mitzvah, which is the Hebrew term for confirmation, when Hymie said to Sollie . . . '

Then you interrupt and say, 'Look here, Rabbi Blue, we've had just about as many Jewish jokes as we can take. We're up to our eyebrows in them! Can't you tell us a nice Gentile one for a change?'

'Sure, why not? Well, there were these two Primitive Methodists going along to a bar mitzvah, which is the Hebrew term for confirmation, when Luther said to Wesley . . . '